ISBN 0-8373-0099-1

C-99   CAREER EXAMINATION SERIES

This is your
PASSBOOK® for...

Building Custodian

Test Preparation Study Guide

Questions & Answers

NLC
NATIONAL LEARNING CORPORATION

Copyright © 2009 by

National Learning Corporation

212 Michael Drive, Syosset, New York 11791

(516) 921-8888
(800) 645-6337
FAX: (516) 921-8743
www.passbooks.com
sales @ passbooks.com
info @ passbooks.com

PRINTED IN THE UNITED STATES OF AMERICA

3 1327 00516 8315

PASSBOOK®
NOTICE

PASSBOOK SERIES®

THE *PASSBOOK SERIES®* has been created to prepare applicants and candidates for the ultimate academic battlefield – the examination room.

At some time in our lives, each and every one of us may be required to take an examination – for validation, matriculation, admission, qualification, registration, certification, or licensure.

Based on the assumption that every applicant or candidate has met the basic formal educational standards, has taken the required number of courses, and read the necessary texts, the *PASSBOOK SERIES®* furnishes the one special preparation which may assure passing with confidence, instead of failing with insecurity. Examination questions – together with answers – are furnished as the basic vehicle for study so that the mysteries of the examination and its compounding difficulties may be eliminated or diminished by a sure method.

This book is meant to help you pass your examination provided that you qualify and are serious in your objective.

The entire field is reviewed through the huge store of content information which is succinctly presented through a provocative and challenging approach – the question-and-answer method.

A climate of success is established by furnishing the correct answers at the end of each test.

You soon learn to recognize types of questions, forms of questions, and patterns of questioning. You may even begin to anticipate expected outcomes.

You perceive that many questions are repeated or adapted so that you can gain acute insights, which may enable you to score many sure points.

You learn how to confront new questions, or types of questions, and to attack them confidently and work out the correct answers.

You note objectives and emphases, and recognize pitfalls and dangers, so that you may make positive educational adjustments.

Moreover, you are kept fully informed in relation to new concepts, methods, practices, and directions in the field.

You discover that you are actually taking the examination all the time: you are preparing for the examination by "taking" an examination, not by reading extraneous and/or supererogatory textbooks.

In short, this PASSBOOK®, used directedly, should be an important factor in helping you to pass your test.

BUILDING CUSTODIAN

DUTIES AND RESPONSIBILITIES

Under general supervision, performs work of moderate difficulty and responsibility in supervising the cleaning, maintaining, and enforcing of safety requirements in large public buildings (other than schools and colleges) and the immediate grounds, or in supervising a considerable force of custodial employees on an assigned shift; performs related work.

EXAMPLES OF TYPICAL TASKS

Is responsible for the cleanliness and maintenance of large public buildings entailing supervision of a considerable force of custodial employees performing such tasks as sweeping, dusting, mopping, polishing, waxing, gathering and disposing of refuse; operating elevators; cleaning walks and snow removal; and maintaining lawns and shrubs. Oversees operation of a low pressure heating system. Inspects building and grounds to note general condition; necessity for repairs; checks work performance; and proper use, cleanliness and storage of tools. May participate in or supervise in making of minor repairs and report conditions requiring services of mechanics. Arranges for and supervises the moving of furniture and equipment. May make acceptability reports on the work performed by maintenance staff and outside contractors. Enforces safety requirements and protects the building and grounds from vandalism. Trains personnel in safe work methods and use of equipment and materials; prepares work schedules; investigates and adjusts complaints about service and personnel. Requisitions fuel; requisitions, stores, issues, and may make estimates of janitorial supplies. Keeps inventories, time sheets and other records; prepares reports on work activities, accidents and unusual conditions.

TESTS

The written test will be of the multiple choice type and may include questions on cleaning and maintenance of buildings and grounds, electrical systems, plumbing systems, building structure, supervision, inspection, public relations, staff development, heating and ventilating, and safety related to large public buildings; and other related areas.

HOW TO TAKE A TEST

I. YOU MUST PASS AN EXAMINATION

A. WHAT EVERY CANDIDATE SHOULD KNOW

Examination applicants often ask us for help in preparing for the written test. What can I study in advance? What kinds of questions will be asked? How will the test be given? How will the papers be graded?

As an applicant for a civil service examination, you may be wondering about some of these things. Our purpose here is to suggest effective methods of advance study and to describe civil service examinations.

Your chances for success on this examination can be increased if you know how to prepare. Those "pre-examination jitters" can be reduced if you know what to expect. You can even experience an adventure in good citizenship if you know why civil service exams are given.

B. WHY ARE CIVIL SERVICE EXAMINATIONS GIVEN?

Civil service examinations are important to you in two ways. As a citizen, you want public jobs filled by employees who know how to do their work. As a job seeker, you want a fair chance to compete for that job on an equal footing with other candidates. The best-known means of accomplishing this two-fold goal is the competitive examination.

Exams are widely publicized throughout the nation. They may be administered for jobs in federal, state, city, municipal, town or village governments or agencies.

Any citizen may apply, with some limitations, such as the age or residence of applicants. Your experience and education may be reviewed to see whether you meet the requirements for the particular examination. When these requirements exist, they are reasonable and applied consistently to all applicants. Thus, a competitive examination may cause you some uneasiness now, but it is your privilege and safeguard.

C. HOW ARE CIVIL SERVICE EXAMS DEVELOPED?

Examinations are carefully written by trained technicians who are specialists in the field known as "psychological measurement," in consultation with recognized authorities in the field of work that the test will cover. These experts recommend the subject matter areas or skills to be tested; only those knowledges or skills important to your success on the job are included. The most reliable books and source materials available are used as references. Together, the experts and technicians judge the difficulty level of the questions.

Test technicians know how to phrase questions so that the problem is clearly stated. Their ethics do not permit "trick" or "catch" questions. Questions may have been tried out on sample groups, or subjected to statistical analysis, to determine their usefulness.

Written tests are often used in combination with performance tests, ratings of training and experience, and oral interviews. All of these measures combine to form the best-known means of finding the right person for the right job.

II. HOW TO PASS THE WRITTEN TEST

A. NATURE OF THE EXAMINATION

To prepare intelligently for civil service examinations, you should know how they differ from school examinations you have taken. In school you were assigned certain definite pages to read or subjects to cover. The examination questions were quite detailed and usually emphasized memory. Civil service exams, on the other hand, try to discover your present ability to perform the duties of a position, plus your potentiality to learn these duties. In other words, a civil service exam attempts to predict how successful you will be. Questions cover such a broad area that they cannot be as minute and detailed as school exam questions.

In the public service similar kinds of work, or positions, are grouped together in one "class." This process is known as *position-classification.* All the positions in a class are paid according to the salary range for that class. One class title covers all of these positions, and they are all tested by the same examination.

B. FOUR BASIC STEPS

1) Study the announcement

How, then, can you know what subjects to study? Our best answer is: "Learn as much as possible about the class of positions for which you've applied." The exam will test the knowledge, skills and abilities needed to do the work.

Your most valuable source of information about the position you want is the official exam announcement. This announcement lists the training and experience qualifications. Check these standards and apply only if you come reasonably close to meeting them.

The brief description of the position in the examination announcement offers some clues to the subjects which will be tested. Think about the job itself. Review the duties in your mind. Can you perform them, or are there some in which you are rusty? Fill in the blank spots in your preparation.

Many jurisdictions preview the written test in the exam announcement by including a section called "Knowledge and Abilities Required," "Scope of the Examination," or some similar heading. Here you will find out specifically what fields will be tested.

2) Review your own background

Once you learn in general what the position is all about, and what you need to know to do the work, ask yourself which subjects you already know fairly well and which need improvement. You may wonder whether to concentrate on improving your strong areas or on building some background in your fields of weakness. When the announcement has specified "some knowledge" or "considerable knowledge," or has used adjectives like "beginning principles of..." or "advanced ... methods," you can get a clue as to the number and difficulty of questions to be asked in any given field. More questions, and hence broader coverage, would be included for those subjects which are more important in the work. Now weigh your strengths and weaknesses against the job requirements and prepare accordingly.

3) Determine the level of the position

Another way to tell how intensively you should prepare is to understand the level of the job for which you are applying. Is it the entering level? In other words, is this the position in which beginners in a field of work are hired? Or is it an intermediate or advanced level? Sometimes this is indicated by such words as "Junior" or "Senior" in the class title. Other jurisdictions use Roman numerals to designate the level – Clerk I, Clerk II, for example. The word "Supervisor" sometimes appears in the title. If the level is not indicated by the title, check the description of duties. Will you be working under very close supervision, or will you have responsibility for independent decisions in this work?

4) Choose appropriate study materials

Now that you know the subjects to be examined and the relative amount of each subject to be covered, you can choose suitable study materials. For beginning level jobs, or even advanced ones, if you have a pronounced weakness in some aspect of your training, read a modern, standard textbook in that field. Be sure it is up to date and has general coverage. Such books are normally available at your library, and the librarian will be glad to help you locate one. For entry-level positions, questions of appropriate difficulty are chosen – neither highly advanced questions, nor those too simple. Such questions require careful thought but not advanced training.

If the position for which you are applying is technical or advanced, you will read more advanced, specialized material. If you are already familiar with the basic principles of your field, elementary textbooks would waste your time. Concentrate on advanced textbooks and technical periodicals. Think through the concepts and review difficult problems in your field.

These are all general sources. You can get more ideas on your own initiative, following these leads. For example, training manuals and publications of the government agency which employs workers in your field can be useful, particularly for technical and professional positions. A letter or visit to the government department involved may result in more specific study suggestions, and certainly will provide you with a more definite idea of the exact nature of the position you are seeking.

III. KINDS OF TESTS

Tests are used for purposes other than measuring knowledge and ability to perform specified duties. For some positions, it is equally important to test ability to make adjustments to new situations or to profit from training. In others, basic mental abilities not dependent on information are essential. Questions which test these things may not appear as pertinent to the duties of the position as those which test for knowledge and information. Yet they are often highly important parts of a fair examination. For very general questions, it is almost impossible to help you direct your study efforts. What we can do is to point out some of the more common of these general abilities needed in public service positions and describe some typical questions.

1) General information

Broad, general information has been found useful for predicting job success in some kinds of work. This is tested in a variety of ways, from vocabulary lists to questions about current events. Basic background in some field of work, such as sociology or economics, may be sampled in a group of questions. Often these are principles which have become familiar to most persons through exposure rather than through formal training. It is difficult to advise you how to study for these questions; being alert to the world around you is our best suggestion.

2) Verbal ability

An example of an ability needed in many positions is verbal or language ability. Verbal ability is, in brief, the ability to use and understand words. Vocabulary and grammar tests are typical measures of this ability. Reading comprehension or paragraph interpretation questions are common in many kinds of civil service tests. You are given a paragraph of written material and asked to find its central meaning.

3) Numerical ability

Number skills can be tested by the familiar arithmetic problem, by checking paired lists of numbers to see which are alike and which are different, or by interpreting charts and graphs. In the latter test, a graph may be printed in the test booklet which you are asked to use as the basis for answering questions.

4) Observation

A popular test for law-enforcement positions is the observation test. A picture is shown to you for several minutes, then taken away. Questions about the picture test your ability to observe both details and larger elements.

5) Following directions

In many positions in the public service, the employee must be able to carry out written instructions dependably and accurately. You may be given a chart with several columns, each column listing a variety of information. The questions require you to carry out directions involving the information given in the chart.

6) Skills and aptitudes

Performance tests effectively measure some manual skills and aptitudes. When the skill is one in which you are trained, such as typing or shorthand, you can practice. These tests are often very much like those given in business school or high school courses. For many of the other skills and aptitudes, however, no short-time preparation can be made. Skills and abilities natural to you or that you have developed throughout your lifetime are being tested.

Many of the general questions just described provide all the data needed to answer the questions and ask you to use your reasoning ability to find the answers. Your best preparation for these tests, as well as for tests of facts and ideas, is to be at your physical and mental best. You, no doubt, have your own methods of getting into an exam-taking mood and keeping "in shape." The next section lists some ideas on this subject.

IV. KINDS OF QUESTIONS

Only rarely is the "essay" question, which you answer in narrative form, used in civil service tests. Civil service tests are usually of the short-answer type. Full instructions for answering these questions will be given to you at the examination. But in case this is your first experience with short-answer questions and separate answer sheets, here is what you need to know:

1) Multiple-choice Questions

Most popular of the short-answer questions is the "multiple choice" or "best answer" question. It can be used, for example, to test for factual knowledge, ability to solve problems or judgment in meeting situations found at work.

A multiple-choice question is normally one of three types—

- It can begin with an incomplete statement followed by several possible endings. You are to find the one ending which *best* completes the statement, although some of the others may not be entirely wrong.
- It can also be a complete statement in the form of a question which is answered by choosing one of the statements listed.
- It can be in the form of a problem – again you select the best answer.

Here is an example of a multiple-choice question with a discussion which should give you some clues as to the method for choosing the right answer:

When an employee has a complaint about his assignment, the action which will *best* help him overcome his difficulty is to
- A. discuss his difficulty with his coworkers
- B. take the problem to the head of the organization
- C. take the problem to the person who gave him the assignment
- D. say nothing to anyone about his complaint

In answering this question, you should study each of the choices to find which is best. Consider choice "A" – Certainly an employee may discuss his complaint with fellow employees, but no change or improvement can result, and the complaint remains unresolved. Choice "B" is a poor choice since the head of the organization probably does not know what assignment you have been given, and taking your problem to him is known as "going over the head" of the supervisor. The supervisor, or person who made the assignment, is the person who can clarify it or correct any injustice. Choice "C" is, therefore, correct. To say nothing, as in choice "D," is unwise. Supervisors have and interest in knowing the problems employees are facing, and the employee is seeking a solution to his problem.

2) True/False Questions

The "true/false" or "right/wrong" form of question is sometimes used. Here a complete statement is given. Your job is to decide whether the statement is right or wrong.

SAMPLE: A person-to-person long-distance telephone call costs less than a station-to-station call to the same city.

This statement is wrong, or false, since person-to-person calls are more expensive.

This is not a complete list of all possible question forms, although most of the others are variations of these common types. You will always get complete directions for answering questions. Be sure you understand *how* to mark your answers – ask questions until you do.

RECORDING YOUR ANSWERS

For an examination with very few applicants, you may be told to record your answers in the test booklet itself. Separate answer sheets are much more common. If this separate answer sheet is to be scored by machine – and this is often the case – it is highly important that you mark your answers correctly in order to get credit.

An electric scoring machine is often used in civil service offices because of the speed with which papers can be scored. Machine-scored answer sheets must be marked with a pencil, which will be given to you. This pencil has a high graphite content which responds to the electric scoring machine. As a matter of fact, stray dots may register as answers, so do not let your pencil rest on the answer sheet while you are pondering the correct answer. Also, if your pencil lead breaks or is otherwise defective, ask for another.

Since the answer sheet will be dropped in a slot in the scoring machine, be careful not to bend the corners or get the paper crumpled.

The answer sheet normally has five vertical columns of numbers, with 30 numbers to a column. These numbers correspond to the question numbers in your test booklet. After each number, going across the page are four or five pairs of dotted lines. These short dotted lines have small letters or numbers above them. The first two pairs may also have a "T" or "F" above the letters. This indicates that the first two pairs only are to be used if the questions are of the true-false type. If the questions are multiple choice, disregard the "T" and "F" and pay attention only to the small letters or numbers.

Answer your questions in the manner of the sample that follows:

32. The largest city in the United States is
    A. Washington, D.C.
    B. New York City
    C. Chicago
    D. Detroit
    E. San Francisco

1) Choose the answer you think is best. (New York City is the largest, so "B" is correct.)
2) Find the row of dotted lines numbered the same as the question you are answering. (Find row number 32)
3) Find the pair of dotted lines corresponding to the answer. (Find the pair of lines under the mark "B.")
4) Make a solid black mark between the dotted lines.

VI. BEFORE THE TEST

Common sense will help you find procedures to follow to get ready for an examination. Too many of us, however, overlook these sensible measures. Indeed, nervousness and fatigue have been found to be the most serious reasons why applicants fail to do their best on civil service tests. Here is a list of reminders:

- Begin your preparation early – Don't wait until the last minute to go scurrying around for books and materials or to find out what the position is all about.
- Prepare continuously – An hour a night for a week is better than an all-night cram session. This has been definitely established. What is more, a night a

week for a month will return better dividends than crowding your study into a shorter period of time.

- Locate the place of the exam – You have been sent a notice telling you when and where to report for the examination. If the location is in a different town or otherwise unfamiliar to you, it would be well to inquire the best route and learn something about the building.
- Relax the night before the test – Allow your mind to rest. Do not study at all that night. Plan some mild recreation or diversion; then go to bed early and get a good night's sleep.
- Get up early enough to make a leisurely trip to the place for the test – This way unforeseen events, traffic snarls, unfamiliar buildings, etc. will not upset you.
- Dress comfortably – A written test is not a fashion show. You will be known by number and not by name, so wear something comfortable.
- Leave excess paraphernalia at home – Shopping bags and odd bundles will get in your way. You need bring only the items mentioned in the official notice you received; usually everything you need is provided. Do not bring reference books to the exam. They will only confuse those last minutes and be taken away from you when in the test room.
- Arrive somewhat ahead of time – If because of transportation schedules you must get there very early, bring a newspaper or magazine to take your mind off yourself while waiting.
- Locate the examination room – When you have found the proper room, you will be directed to the seat or part of the room where you will sit. Sometimes you are given a sheet of instructions to read while you are waiting. Do not fill out any forms until you are told to do so; just read them and be prepared.
- Relax and prepare to listen to the instructions
- If you have any physical problem that may keep you from doing your best, be sure to tell the test administrator. If you are sick or in poor health, you really cannot do your best on the exam. You can come back and take the test some other time.

VII. AT THE TEST

The day of the test is here and you have the test booklet in your hand. The temptation to get going is very strong. Caution! There is more to success than knowing the right answers. You must know how to identify your papers and understand variations in the type of short-answer question used in this particular examination. Follow these suggestions for maximum results from your efforts:

1) Cooperate with the monitor

The test administrator has a duty to create a situation in which you can be as much at ease as possible. He will give instructions, tell you when to begin, check to see that you are marking your answer sheet correctly, and so on. He is not there to guard you, although he will see that your competitors do not take unfair advantage. He wants to help you do your best.

2) Listen to all instructions

Don't jump the gun! Wait until you understand all directions. In most civil service tests you get more time than you need to answer the questions. So don't be in a hurry.

Read each word of instructions until you clearly understand the meaning. Study the examples, listen to all announcements and follow directions. Ask questions if you do not understand what to do.

3) Identify your papers

Civil service exams are usually identified by number only. You will be assigned a number; you must not put your name on your test papers. Be sure to copy your number correctly. Since more than one exam may be given, copy your exact examination title.

4) Plan your time

Unless you are told that a test is a "speed" or "rate of work" test, speed itself is usually not important. Time enough to answer all the questions will be provided, but this does not mean that you have all day. An overall time limit has been set. Divide the total time (in minutes) by the number of questions to determine the approximate time you have for each question.

5) Do not linger over difficult questions

If you come across a difficult question, mark it with a paper clip (useful to have along) and come back to it when you have been through the booklet. One caution if you do this – be sure to skip a number on your answer sheet as well. Check often to be sure that you have not lost your place and that you are marking in the row numbered the same as the question you are answering.

6) Read the questions

Be sure you know what the question asks! Many capable people are unsuccessful because they failed to *read* the questions correctly.

7) Answer all questions

Unless you have been instructed that a penalty will be deducted for incorrect answers, it is better to guess than to omit a question.

8) Speed tests

It is often better NOT to guess on speed tests. It has been found that on timed tests people are tempted to spend the last few seconds before time is called in marking answers at random – without even reading them – in the hope of picking up a few extra points. To discourage this practice, the instructions may warn you that your score will be "corrected" for guessing. That is, a penalty will be applied. The incorrect answers will be deducted from the correct ones, or some other penalty formula will be used.

9) Review your answers

If you finish before time is called, go back to the questions you guessed or omitted to give them further thought. Review other answers if you have time.

10) Return your test materials

If you are ready to leave before others have finished or time is called, take ALL your materials to the monitor and leave quietly. Never take any test material with you. The monitor can discover whose papers are not complete, and taking a test booklet may be grounds for disqualification.

VIII. EXAMINATION TECHNIQUES

1) Read the general instructions carefully. These are usually printed on the first page of the exam booklet. As a rule, these instructions refer to the timing of the examination; the fact that you should not start work until the signal and must stop work at a signal, etc. If there are any *special* instructions, such as a choice of questions to be answered, make sure that you note this instruction carefully.

2) When you are ready to start work on the examination, that is as soon as the signal has been given, read the instructions to each question booklet, underline any key words or phrases, such as *least, best, outline, describe* and the like. In this way you will tend to answer as requested rather than discover on reviewing your paper that you *listed without describing*, that you selected the *worst* choice rather than the *best* choice, etc.

3) If the examination is of the objective or multiple-choice type – that is, each question will also give a series of possible answers: A, B, C or D, and you are called upon to select the best answer and write the letter next to that answer on your answer paper – it is advisable to start answering each question in turn. There may be anywhere from 50 to 100 such questions in the three or four hours allotted and you can see how much time would be taken if you read through all the questions before beginning to answer any. Furthermore, if you come across a question or group of questions which you know would be difficult to answer, it would undoubtedly affect your handling of all the other questions.

4) If the examination is of the essay type and contains but a few questions, it is a moot point as to whether you should read all the questions before starting to answer any one. Of course, if you are given a choice – say five out of seven and the like – then it is essential to read all the questions so you can eliminate the two that are most difficult. If, however, you are asked to answer all the questions, there may be danger in trying to answer the easiest one first because you may find that you will spend too much time on it. The best technique is to answer the first question, then proceed to the second, etc.

5) Time your answers. Before the exam begins, write down the time it started, then add the time allowed for the examination and write down the time it must be completed, then divide the time available somewhat as follows:
   - If 3-1/2 hours are allowed, that would be 210 minutes. If you have 80 objective-type questions, that would be an average of 2-1/2 minutes per question. Allow yourself no more than 2 minutes per question, or a total of 160 minutes, which will permit about 50 minutes to review.
   - If for the time allotment of 210 minutes there are 7 essay questions to answer, that would average about 30 minutes a question. Give yourself only 25 minutes per question so that you have about 35 minutes to review.

6) The most important instruction is to *read each question* and make sure you know what is wanted. The second most important instruction is to *time yourself properly* so that you answer every question. The third most

important instruction is to *answer every question*. Guess if you have to but include something for each question. Remember that you will receive no credit for a blank and will probably receive some credit if you write something in answer to an essay question. If you guess a letter – say "B" for a multiple-choice question – you may have guessed right. If you leave a blank as an answer to a multiple-choice question, the examiners may respect your feelings but it will not add a point to your score. Some exams may penalize you for wrong answers, so in such cases *only*, you may not want to guess unless you have some basis for your answer.

7) Suggestions
   a. Objective-type questions
      1. Examine the question booklet for proper sequence of pages and questions
      2. Read all instructions carefully
      3. Skip any question which seems too difficult; return to it after all other questions have been answered
      4. Apportion your time properly; do not spend too much time on any single question or group of questions
      5. Note and underline key words – *all, most, fewest, least, best, worst, same, opposite*, etc.
      6. Pay particular attention to negatives
      7. Note unusual option, e.g., unduly long, short, complex, different or similar in content to the body of the question
      8. Observe the use of "hedging" words – *probably, may, most likely*, etc.
      9. Make sure that your answer is put next to the same number as the question
     10. Do not second-guess unless you have good reason to believe the second answer is definitely more correct
     11. Cross out original answer if you decide another answer is more accurate; do not erase until you are ready to hand your paper in
     12. Answer all questions; guess unless instructed otherwise
     13. Leave time for review

   b. Essay questions
      1. Read each question carefully
      2. Determine exactly what is wanted. Underline key words or phrases.
      3. Decide on outline or paragraph answer
      4. Include many different points and elements unless asked to develop any one or two points or elements
      5. Show impartiality by giving pros and cons unless directed to select one side only
      6. Make and write down any assumptions you find necessary to answer the questions
      7. Watch your English, grammar, punctuation and choice of words
      8. Time your answers; don't crowd material

8) Answering the essay question

Most essay questions can be answered by framing the specific response around several key words or ideas. Here are a few such key words or ideas:

M's: manpower, materials, methods, money, management
P's: purpose, program, policy, plan, procedure, practice, problems, pitfalls, personnel, public relations

    a. Six basic steps in handling problems:
1. Preliminary plan and background development
2. Collect information, data and facts
3. Analyze and interpret information, data and facts
4. Analyze and develop solutions as well as make recommendations
5. Prepare report and sell recommendations
6. Install recommendations and follow up effectiveness

    b. Pitfalls to avoid
1. *Taking things for granted* – A statement of the situation does not necessarily imply that each of the elements is necessarily true; for example, a complaint may be invalid and biased so that all that can be taken for granted is that a complaint has been registered
2. *Considering only one side of a situation* – Wherever possible, indicate several alternatives and then point out the reasons you selected the best one
3. *Failing to indicate follow up* – Whenever your answer indicates action on your part, make certain that you will take proper follow-up action to see how successful your recommendations, procedures or actions turn out to be
4. *Taking too long in answering any single question* – Remember to time your answers properly

IX. AFTER THE TEST

Scoring procedures differ in detail among civil service jurisdictions although the general principles are the same. Whether the papers are hand-scored or graded by machine we have described, they are nearly always graded by number. That is, the person who marks the paper knows only the number – never the name – of the applicant. Not until all the papers have been graded will they be matched with names. If other tests, such as training and experience or oral interview ratings have been given, scores will be combined. Different parts of the examination usually have different weights. For example, the written test might count 60 percent of the final grade, and a rating of training and experience 40 percent. In many jurisdictions, veterans will have a certain number of points added to their grades.

After the final grade has been determined, the names are placed in grade order and an eligible list is established. There are various methods for resolving ties between those who get the same final grade – probably the most common is to place first the name of the person whose application was received first. Job offers are made from the eligible list in the order the names appear on it. You will be notified of your grade and your rank as soon as all these computations have been made. This will be done as rapidly as possible.

People who are found to meet the requirements in the announcement are called "eligibles." Their names are put on a list of eligible candidates. An eligible's chances of getting a job depend on how high he stands on this list and how fast agencies are filling jobs from the list.

When a job is to be filled from a list of eligibles, the agency asks for the names of people on the list of eligibles for that job. When the civil service commission receives this request, it sends to the agency the names of the three people highest on this list. Or, if the job to be filled has specialized requirements, the office sends the agency the names of the top three persons who meet these requirements from the general list.

The appointing officer makes a choice from among the three people whose names were sent to him. If the selected person accepts the appointment, the names of the others are put back on the list to be considered for future openings.

That is the rule in hiring from all kinds of eligible lists, whether they are for typist, carpenter, chemist, or something else. For every vacancy, the appointing officer has his choice of any one of the top three eligibles on the list. This explains why the person whose name is on top of the list sometimes does not get an appointment when some of the persons lower on the list do. If the appointing officer chooses the second or third eligible, the No. 1 eligible does not get a job at once, but stays on the list until he is appointed or the list is terminated.

X. HOW TO PASS THE INTERVIEW TEST

The examination for which you applied requires an oral interview test. You have already taken the written test and you are now being called for the interview test – the final part of the formal examination.

You may think that it is not possible to prepare for an interview test and that there are no procedures to follow during an interview. Our purpose is to point out some things you can do in advance that will help you and some good rules to follow and pitfalls to avoid while you are being interviewed.

What is an interview supposed to test?

The written examination is designed to test the technical knowledge and competence of the candidate; the oral is designed to evaluate intangible qualities, not readily measured otherwise, and to establish a list showing the relative fitness of each candidate – as measured against his competitors – for the position sought. Scoring is not on the basis of "right" and "wrong," but on a sliding scale of values ranging from "not passable" to "outstanding." As a matter of fact, it is possible to achieve a relatively low score without a single "incorrect" answer because of evident weakness in the qualities being measured.

Occasionally, an examination may consist entirely of an oral test – either an individual or a group oral. In such cases, information is sought concerning the technical knowledges and abilities of the candidate, since there has been no written examination for this purpose. More commonly, however, an oral test is used to supplement a written examination.

Who conducts interviews?

The composition of oral boards varies among different jurisdictions. In nearly all, a representative of the personnel department serves as chairman. One of the members of the board may be a representative of the department in which the candidate would work. In some cases, "outside experts" are used, and, frequently, a businessman or some other representative of the general public is asked to serve. Labor and management or other special groups may be represented. The aim is to secure the services of experts in the appropriate field.

However the board is composed, it is a good idea (and not at all improper or unethical) to ascertain in advance of the interview who the members are and what groups they represent. When you are introduced to them, you will have some idea of their backgrounds and interests, and at least you will not stutter and stammer over their names.

What should be done before the interview?

While knowledge about the board members is useful and takes some of the surprise element out of the interview, there is other preparation which is more substantive. It *is* possible to prepare for an oral interview – in several ways:

1) Keep a copy of your application and review it carefully before the interview

This may be the only document before the oral board, and the starting point of the interview. Know what education and experience you have listed there, and the sequence and dates of all of it. Sometimes the board will ask you to review the highlights of your experience for them; you should not have to hem and haw doing it.

2) Study the class specification and the examination announcement

Usually, the oral board has one or both of these to guide them. The qualities, characteristics or knowledges required by the position sought are stated in these documents. They offer valuable clues as to the nature of the oral interview. For example, if the job involves supervisory responsibilities, the announcement will usually indicate that knowledge of modern supervisory methods and the qualifications of the candidate as a supervisor will be tested. If so, you can expect such questions, frequently in the form of a hypothetical situation which you are expected to solve. NEVER go into an oral without knowledge of the duties and responsibilities of the job you seek.

3) Think through each qualification required

Try to visualize the kind of questions you would ask if you were a board member. How well could you answer them? Try especially to appraise your own knowledge and background in each area, *measured against the job sought*, and identify any areas in which you are weak. Be critical and realistic – do not flatter yourself.

4) Do some general reading in areas in which you feel you may be weak

For example, if the job involves supervision and your past experience has NOT, some general reading in supervisory methods and practices, particularly in the field of human relations, might be useful. Do NOT study agency procedures or detailed manuals. The oral board will be testing your understanding and capacity, not your memory.

5) Get a good night's sleep and watch your general health and mental attitude

You will want a clear head at the interview. Take care of a cold or any other minor ailment, and of course, no hangovers.

What should be done on the day of the interview?

Now comes the day of the interview itself. Give yourself plenty of time to get there. Plan to arrive somewhat ahead of the scheduled time, particularly if your appointment is in the fore part of the day. If a previous candidate fails to appear, the board might be ready for you a bit early. By early afternoon an oral board is almost invariably behind schedule if there are many candidates, and you may have to wait.

Take along a book or magazine to read, or your application to review, but leave any extraneous material in the waiting room when you go in for your interview. In any event, relax and compose yourself.

The matter of dress is important. The board is forming impressions about you – from your experience, your manners, your attitude, and your appearance. Give your personal appearance careful attention. Dress your best, but not your flashiest. Choose conservative, appropriate clothing, and be sure it is immaculate. This is a business interview, and your appearance should indicate that you regard it as such. Besides, being well groomed and properly dressed will help boost your confidence.

Sooner or later, someone will call your name and escort you into the interview room. *This is it.* From here on you are on your own. It is too late for any more preparation. But remember, you asked for this opportunity to prove your fitness, and you are here because your request was granted.

What happens when you go in?

The usual sequence of events will be as follows: The clerk (who is often the board stenographer) will introduce you to the chairman of the oral board, who will introduce you to the other members of the board. Acknowledge the introductions before you sit down. Do not be surprised if you find a microphone facing you or a stenotypist sitting by. Oral interviews are usually recorded in the event of an appeal or other review.

Usually the chairman of the board will open the interview by reviewing the highlights of your education and work experience from your application – primarily for the benefit of the other members of the board, as well as to get the material into the record. Do not interrupt or comment unless there is an error or significant misinterpretation; if that is the case, do not hesitate. But do not quibble about insignificant matters. Also, he will usually ask you some question about your education, experience or your present job – partly to get you to start talking and to establish the interviewing "rapport." He may start the actual questioning, or turn it over to one of the other members. Frequently, each member undertakes the questioning on a particular area, one in which he is perhaps most competent, so you can expect each member to participate in the examination. Because time is limited, you may also expect some rather abrupt switches in the direction the questioning takes, so do not be upset by it. Normally, a board member will not pursue a single line of questioning unless he discovers a particular strength or weakness.

After each member has participated, the chairman will usually ask whether any member has any further questions, then will ask you if you have anything you wish to add. Unless you are expecting this question, it may floor you. Worse, it may start you off on an extended, extemporaneous speech. The board is not usually seeking more information. The question is principally to offer you a last opportunity to present further qualifications or to indicate that you have nothing to add. So, if you feel that a significant qualification or characteristic has been overlooked, it is proper to point it out in a sentence or so. Do not compliment the board on the thoroughness of their examination – they have been sketchy, and you know it. If you wish, merely say, "No thank you, I have nothing further to add." This is a point where you can "talk yourself out" of a good impression or fail to present an important bit of information. Remember, *you close the interview yourself.*

The chairman will then say, "That is all, Mr. _____, thank you." Do not be startled; the interview is over, and quicker than you think. Thank him, gather your belongings and take your leave. Save your sigh of relief for the other side of the door.

How to put your best foot forward

Throughout this entire process, you may feel that the board individually and collectively is trying to pierce your defenses, seek out your hidden weaknesses and embarrass and confuse you. Actually, this is not true. They are obliged to make an appraisal of your qualifications for the job you are seeking, and they want to see you in your best light. Remember, they must interview all candidates and a non-cooperative candidate may become a failure in spite of their best efforts to bring out his qualifications. Here are 15 suggestions that will help you:

1) Be natural – Keep your attitude confident, not cocky

If you are not confident that you can do the job, do not expect the board to be. Do not apologize for your weaknesses, try to bring out your strong points. The board is interested in a positive, not negative, presentation. Cockiness will antagonize any board member and make him wonder if you are covering up a weakness by a false show of strength.

2) Get comfortable, but don't lounge or sprawl

Sit erectly but not stiffly. A careless posture may lead the board to conclude that you are careless in other things, or at least that you are not impressed by the importance of the occasion. Either conclusion is natural, even if incorrect. Do not fuss with your clothing, a pencil or an ashtray. Your hands may occasionally be useful to emphasize a point; do not let them become a point of distraction.

3) Do not wisecrack or make small talk

This is a serious situation, and your attitude should show that you consider it as such. Further, the time of the board is limited – they do not want to waste it, and neither should you.

4) Do not exaggerate your experience or abilities

In the first place, from information in the application or other interviews and sources, the board may know more about you than you think. Secondly, you probably will not get away with it. An experienced board is rather adept at spotting such a situation, so do not take the chance.

5) If you know a board member, do not make a point of it, yet do not hide it

Certainly you are not fooling him, and probably not the other members of the board. Do not try to take advantage of your acquaintanceship – it will probably do you little good.

6) Do not dominate the interview

Let the board do that. They will give you the clues – do not assume that you have to do all the talking. Realize that the board has a number of questions to ask you, and do not try to take up all the interview time by showing off your extensive knowledge of the answer to the first one.

7) Be attentive

You only have 20 minutes or so, and you should keep your attention at its sharpest throughout. When a member is addressing a problem or question to you, give him your undivided attention. Address your reply principally to him, but do not exclude the other board members.

8) Do not interrupt

A board member may be stating a problem for you to analyze. He will ask you a question when the time comes. Let him state the problem, and wait for the question.

9) Make sure you understand the question

Do not try to answer until you are sure what the question is. If it is not clear, restate it in your own words or ask the board member to clarify it for you. However, do not haggle about minor elements.

10) Reply promptly but not hastily

A common entry on oral board rating sheets is "candidate responded readily," or "candidate hesitated in replies." Respond as promptly and quickly as you can, but do not jump to a hasty, ill-considered answer.

11) Do not be peremptory in your answers

A brief answer is proper – but do not fire your answer back. That is a losing game from your point of view. The board member can probably ask questions much faster than you can answer them.

12) Do not try to create the answer you think the board member wants

He is interested in what kind of mind you have and how it works – not in playing games. Furthermore, he can usually spot this practice and will actually grade you down on it.

13) Do not switch sides in your reply merely to agree with a board member

Frequently, a member will take a contrary position merely to draw you out and to see if you are willing and able to defend your point of view. Do not start a debate, yet do not surrender a good position. If a position is worth taking, it is worth defending.

14) Do not be afraid to admit an error in judgment if you are shown to be wrong

The board knows that you are forced to reply without any opportunity for careful consideration. Your answer may be demonstrably wrong. If so, admit it and get on with the interview.

15) Do not dwell at length on your present job

The opening question may relate to your present assignment. Answer the question but do not go into an extended discussion. You are being examined for a *new* job, not your present one. As a matter of fact, try to phrase ALL your answers in terms of the job for which you are being examined.

Basis of Rating

Probably you will forget most of these "do's" and "don'ts" when you walk into the oral interview room. Even remembering them all will not ensure you a passing grade. Perhaps you did not have the qualifications in the first place. But remembering them will help you to put your best foot forward, without treading on the toes of the board members.

Rumor and popular opinion to the contrary notwithstanding, an oral board wants you to make the best appearance possible. They know you are under pressure – but they also want to see how you respond to it as a guide to what your reaction would be under the pressures of the job you seek. They will be influenced by the degree of poise you display, the personal traits you show and the manner in which you respond.

EXAMINATION SECTION

EXAMINATION SECTION

TEST 1

DIRECTIONS: Each question or incomplete statement is followed by several suggested answers or completions. Select the one that BEST answers the question or completes the statement. *PRINT THE LETTER OF THE CORRECT ANSWER IN THE SPACE AT THE RIGHT.*

1. The KEY figure in any custodial safety program is the   1.____
    A. custodian   B. cleaner   C. mayor   D. commissioner

2. A custodian must inspect or have a maintenance man inspect   2.____
   every window cleaner's safety belt AT LEAST
    A. each time the windows are washed
    B. once a month
    C. once a year
    D. once every second year

3. A custodian's written instruction to his staff on the   3.____
   subject of security in public buildings should include
   instructions to
    A. exclude the public at all times
    B. admit the public at all times
    C. admit the public only if they are neat and well-dressed
    D. admit the public during specified hours

4. A custodian in charge of a building who is normally on   4.____
   duty during the daytime hours in a building which is
   cleaned at night should
    A. never make night inspections since he is not
       responsible for the cleanliness of the building
    B. make night inspections at least once a year
    C. never make night inspections because the cleaners
       will think he is spying on them
    D. make night inspections at least twice a month

5. The employee MOST likely to find the nests and runways   5.____
   of roaches and vermin in a building is a
    A. maintenance man   B. night cleaner
    C. building custodian   D. stationary fireman

6. When mopping, the pails containing the cleaning solutions   6.____
   should be
    A. slid along the floor to avoid injury due to lifting
    B. kept off the floor preferably on a rolling platform
    C. shifted from place to place using the mop
    D. equipped with a spigot for applying the mopping
       solution

7. Of the following, the item that is considered a concrete   7.____
   floor sealer is
    A. water wax   B. sodium hypochlorite
    C. sodium silicate   D. linseed oil

8. A material COMMONLY used in detergents is   8.___
   A. rock salt   B. Glauber's salt
   C. tri-sodium phosphate   D. monosodium glutamate

9. A disinfectant material is one that will   9.___
   A. kill germs
   B. dissolve soil and stop odors
   C. give a clean odor and cover a disagreeable odor
   D. prevent soil buildup

10. When scrubbing a wooden floor, it is ADVISABLE to   10.___
   A. flood the surface with the cleaning solution in order
      to float the soil out of all crevices
   B. hose off the loosened soil before starting the
      scrubbing operation
   C. pick up the used solution as soon as possible
   D. mix a mild acid with the cleaning solution in order
      to clean the surface quickly

11. Before starting a wall washing operation, it is BEST to 11.___
   A. check the temperature of the water
   B. soak the sponge to be used
   C. check the pH of the mixed cleaning solution
   D. dust the wall to be washed

12. Of the following, the MOST nearly correct statement   12.___
regarding the economical operation of the heating system
in a building is that
   A. the heat should always be shut down at 4 P.M. and
      turned on at 8 A.M.
   B. the heat should be shut down only over the weekend
   C. it is best to keep the heat on at all times so that
      the number of complaints are kept to a minimum
   D. the times at which the heat is shut down and turned
      on should be varied depending on the prevailing
      outdoor temperature

13. A floor made of marble or granite chips imbedded in cement 13.___
is USUALLY called
   A. terrazzo   B. linoleum   C. palmetto   D. parquet

14. In a 4-wire, 3-phase electrical supply system, the voltage 14.___
between one phase and ground used for the lighting load
is MOST NEARLY
   A. 440   B. 230   C. 208   D. 115

15. Of the following, the one that takes the place of a fuse 15.___
in an electrical circuit is a
   A. transformer   B. circuit breaker
   C. condenser   D. knife switch

16. Gas bills are USUALLY computed on the basis of   16.___
   A. cubic feet B. gallons   C. pounds   D. kilowatts

17. An operating oil-fired steam boiler explosion may some-   17.___
    times be caused by
    A. carrying too high a water level in the boiler
    B. inadequate purging of combustion chamber between fires
    C. overfiring the boiler
    D. carrying too high an oil temperature

18. The one of the following commercial sizes of anthracite   18.___
    which is the LARGEST in size is
    A. stove   B. chestnut   C. pea   D. rice

19. Assume that six windows of a public building facing one   19.___
    street have been consistently broken by boys playing ball
    after hours and over weekends.
    The BEST solution to this problem is to
    A. post a *no ball playing* sign on the wall
    B. erect protective screening outside the six windows
    C. post a guard on weekend patrol duty
    D. request special weekend police protection for the property

20. The BEST method or tool to use for cleaning dust from an   20.___
    unplastered cinderblock wall is
    A. a tampico brush with stock cleaning solution
    B. a vacuum cleaner
    C. water under pressure from hose and nozzle
    D. a feather duster

21. Of the following, the LARGEST individual item of expense   21.___
    in operating a public building is generally the cost of
    A. cleaning   B. heating fuel
    C. electricity   D. elevator service

22. The CHIEF purpose for changing the handle of a floor   22.___
    brush from one side of the brush block to the other side
    is to
    A. allow the janitor to change hands
    B. make both sides of the brush equally dirty
    C. give both sides of the brush equal wear
    D. change the angle of sweeping

23. Of the following, the weight of mop MOST likely used in   23.___
    the nightly mopping of corridors, halls, or lobbies is
    ____ ounce.
    A. 8   B. 16   C. 24   D. 50

24. After a sweeping assignment is completed, floor brushes   24.___
    should be stored
    A. in a pan of water
    B. by hanging the brushes on pegs or nails
    C. by piling the brushes on each other carefully
    D. in a normal sweeping position, bristles resting on
       the floor

25. Nylon treated scrubbing discs   25.___
    A. require more water than scrubbing brushes
    B. require more detergent solution than scrubbing brushes
    C. must be used with cold water only
    D. are generally more effective than steel wool pads

26. Of the following, the BEST material to use to clean
exterior bronze is
    A. pumice
    B. paste wax
    C. wire wheel on portable buffer
    D. lemon oil polish
26.____

27. The use of trisodium phosphate in cleaning polished
marble should be AVOIDED because it
    A. may cause spalling
    B. discolors the surface of the marble
    C. builds up a slick surface on the marble
    D. pits the glazed surface and bleaches the marble
27.____

28. The floor area, in square feet, on which a properly
treated dustless sweeping cloth can be used before the
cloth must be washed is
    A. 500 - 1000   B. 2000 - 3000
    C. 4000 - 6000   D. 8000 - 10000
28.____

29. A cleaning woman working a six-hour shift should be able
to cover (clean) ____ Gilbert work units.
    A. 100-200   B. 400-500   C. 1100-1200   D. 6000-7000
29.____

30. An *incipient* fire is one which
    A. has just started and can be readily extinguished using
        an ordinary hand extinguisher
    B. occurs only in motor vehicles
    C. is burning out of control in a storeroom
    D. is a banked coal fire
30.____

31. Maintaining room temperature at 75°F in the winter time
will increase fuel consumption above the amount needed to
maintain 70°F by APPROXIMATELY
    A. 5%   B. 10%   C. 15%   D. 20%
31.____

32. Of the following, the one which represents the BEST practical combustion condition in an oil-fired low pressure
steam plant is ____ stack temperature.
    A. 8% CO_2 - 500°F   B. 13% CO_2 - 400°F
    C. 10% CO_2 - 700°F   D. 6% CO_2 - 400°F
32.____

33. An office has floor dimensions of 16 ft. 6 in. wide by
22 ft. 0 in. long.
The floor area of this office, in square feet, is MOST NEARLY
    A. 143   B. 263   C. 363   D. 463
33.____

34. Dollies are USUALLY used
    A. as convenient platforms upon which to store items
    B. as ornamental protective covers
    C. to raise items to the required level
    D. to transport items from one place to another
34.____

35. When lifting a heavy object from a table, which of the
following rules is it MOST important to observe?
    A. Do not bend your knees.
    B. Do not stand too close to the object.
35.____

C. Keep your back straight.
D. Keep your shoulder level with the object.

36. The FIRST objective of all fire prevention is   36.___
    A. confining fire to a limited area
    B. safeguarding life against fire
    C. reducing insurance rates
    D. preventing property damage

37. A custodian should know the equipment used in his work   37.___
    well enough to
    A. make any repairs which might be needed
    B. know what parts to remove in case of breakdown
    C. anticipate any reasonable possibility of a breakdown
    D. know all the lubricants specified by the manufacturer

38. The PRIMARY responsibility of a supervising custodian is   38.___
    to
    A. make friends of all subordinates
    B. search for new methods of doing the work
    C. win the respect of his superior
    D. get the work done properly within a reasonable time

39. When a custodian believes that the work of a subordinate   39.___
    is below standard, he should
    A. assign the employee to work that is considered
       undesirable
    B. do nothing immediately in the hope that the employee
       will bring his work up to standard without any help
       from the supervisor
    C. reduce the privileges of the employee at once
    D. discuss it as soon as possible with the employee

40. An office worker frequently complains to the custodian   40.___
    that her office is poorly illuminated.
    The BEST action for the custodian to follow is to
    A. ignore the complaints as those of an habitual crank
    B. inform the worker that illumination is a fixed item
       built into the building originally and evidently is
       the result of faulty planning by the architect
    C. request a licensed electrician to install additional
       ceiling lights
    D. investigate for faulty illumination features in the
       room, such as dirty lamp globes and incorrect lamp
       wattages

KEY (CORRECT ANSWERS)

1. A	11. D	21. A	31. D
2. C	12. D	22. C	32. B
3. D	13. A	23. C	33. C
4. D	14. D	24. B	34. D
5. B	15. B	25. D	35. C
6. B	16. A	26. D	36. B
7. C	17. B	27. A	37. C
8. C	18. A	28. C	38. D
9. A	19. B	29. C	39. D
10. C	20. B	30. A	40. D

TEST 2

DIRECTIONS: Each question or incomplete statement is followed by several suggested answers or completions. Select the one that BEST answers the question or completes the statement. *PRINT THE LETTER OF THE CORRECT ANSWER IN THE SPACE AT THE RIGHT.*

1. Of the following, the MOST important reason for the custodian to plan work schedules for men under his supervision is that   1.___
   A. emergency situations can easily be handled if they should arise
   B. it insures that essential operations will be adequately covered
   C. the men will be more satisfied if a routine is established
   D. the relationship between the supervisor and his subordinate will be clarified

2. Sealers for open-grained wood floors should NOT contain linseed oil because   2.___
   A. the linseed oil would damage the wood fibers
   B. the linseed oil would deteriorate mop strands
   C. water wax would penetrate the linseed oil sealer and rot the wood
   D. linseed oil on wood takes too long to dry satisfactorily before a floor finish could be applied

3. When washing painted wall areas by hand, a man should be expected to wash each hour an area, in square feet, equal to   3.___
   A. 75-125   B. 150-300   C. 400-600   D. 750-1000

4. Of the following, the one that is MOST desirable to use in dusting furniture is a   4.___
   A. feather duster   B. paper towel
   C. counter brush   D. soft cotton cloth

5. The one of the following floor types on which oily sweeping compound may be used is   5.___
   A. vinyl tile B. concrete   C. linoleum   D. terrazzo

6. A steam heating system where the steam and condensate flow in the same pipe is called a ____ system.   6.___
   A. one pipe gravity return B. sub-atmospheric
   C. vacuum return   D. zone control

7. A test of a boiler by applying pressure equal to or greater than the maximum working pressure is called a ____ test.   7.___
   A. hydrostatic   B. barometric
   C. hygroscopic   D. gyroscopic

8. A stack switch as used with an oil burner   8.___
    A. shuts down the burner in case of non-ignition
    B. shuts down the burner in case of high stack temperatures
    C. controls the flow of secondary air
    D. operates the barometric damper

9. The vertical pipes leading from the steam mains to the   9.___
   radiators are called
    A. drip lines   B. risers
    C. radiant coils   D. expansion joints

10. Fuel oil storage tanks are equipped with vents.   10.___
    The purpose of these vents is to
    A. make tank soundings   B. check oil flash points
    C. fill the fuel tanks   D. allow air to mix

11. A compound gauge in a boiler room   11.___
    A. measures steam and water pressure
    B. shows the quantity of boiler treatment compound on hand
    C. measures pressures above and below atmospheric pressure
    D. indicates the degree of compounding in a steam engine

12. Of the following, the CHIEF purpose of insulating steam   12.___
   lines is to
    A. prevent loss of heat
    B. protect people from being burned by them
    C. prevent leaks
    D. protect the pipes against corrosion

13. The MOST important function of thermostatic traps on   13.___
   radiators is to
    A. regulate the heat given off by the radiator
    B. remove water and air from the radiator
    C. assist the steam pressure in filling the radiator
    D. maintain a vacuum within the radiator

14. The designation 1/8 - 27 N.P.T. USUALLY indicates   14.___
    A. machine screw thread   B. pipe thread
    C. spur gear size   D. sprocket chain size

15. The size of a chisel is determined by its   15.___
    A. length   B. width   C. pitch   D. height

16. The cause of paint blisters is USUALLY   16.___
    A. moisture under the paint coat
    B. too thick a coat of paint
    C. too much oil in paint
    D. the plaster pores not sealed properly

17. A wood-framed picture is to be attached to a plaster and   17.___
   hollow tile wall.
   Of the following, the proper installation would include
   the use of
    A. wire cut nails
    B. miracle glue
    C. expansion shields and screws
    D. self-tapping screws

18. The PROPER tool or method to use for driving a finish nail   18.___
    to the depth necessary for puttying when installing wood
    trim is
      A. a countersink
      B. another nail of the same diameter
      C. a nail set
      D. a center punch

19. Faucet leakage in a large building is BEST controlled by   19.___
    periodic
      A. faucet replacement
      B. addition of a sealing compound to the water supply
      C. packing replacement
      D. faucet inspection and repair

20. Escutcheons are USUALLY located   20.___
      A. on kitchen cabinet drawers
      B. on windows
      C. around pipes, to cover pipe sleeve openings
      D. around armored electric cable going into a gem box

21. It is ADVISABLE to remove broken bulbs from light sockets   21.___
    with
      A. a wooden or hard rubber wedge
      B. pliers
      C. a hammer and chisel
      D. a fuse puller

22. A room 20' x 25' in area with a ceiling height of 9'6" is   22.___
    to be painted. One gallon of paint will cover 400 square
    feet.
    The MINIMUM number of gallons necessary to give the four
    walls and the ceiling one coat of paint is
      A. 2   B. 3   C. 4   D. 5

23. Of the following, the ones on which gaskets are MOST   23.___
    likely to be used are
      A. threaded pipe plugs
      B. cast iron pipe nipples
      C. flanged pipe fittings
      D. threaded cast iron reducing tees

24. If a 110 volt lamp were used on a 220 volt circuit, the   24.___
      A. fuse would burn out   B. lamp would burn out
      C. line would overheat   D. lamp would flicker

25. The third prong on the plug of portable electric power   25.___
    tools of recent manufacture is for
      A. using the tool on a 3-phase power outlet
      B. eliminating interference in radio or television sets
      C. grounding the tool as a safety precaution
      D. using the tool on direct current circuits

26. When changing brushes on a scrubbing machine, of the   26.___
    following, the FIRST step to take is to
      A. lock the switch in the *off* position

    B. be sure the power cable electric plug supplying the
       machine is disconnected from the wall outlet
    C. place the machine on top of the positioned brushes
    D. dip the brushes in water

27. In cleaning away branches that have been broken off as a   27.___
result of a severe storm, one of your men comes in contact
with a live electric line and falls unconscious.
After having removed him from contact, the FIRST thing to
be done is to
    A. send for an inhalator to revive him
    B. administer mouth-to-mouth resuscitation
    C. search for the switch to prevent any other such cases
    D. loosen his clothing and begin rubbing his forehead
       to restore circulation

28. Of the following, the MOST effective way to reduce waste   28.___
in cleaning equipment and tools is by
    A. requiring a worn brush or broom to be returned before
       issuing a new one
    B. requiring the cleaners to use all cleaning tools for
       specific periods of time
    C. keeping careful records of how frequently cleaning
       equipment and tools are issued to cleaners
    D. making sure that cleaners use the tools properly

29. A window cleaner should carefully examine his safety belt   29.___
    A. once a week
    B. before he puts it on each time
    C. once a month
    D. once before he enters a building

30. One of your cleaners was injured as a result of slipping   30.___
on an oily floor.
This type of accident is MOST likely due to
    A. defective equipment
    B. the physical condition of the cleaner
    C. failure to use proper safety appliances
    D. poor housekeeping

31. One important use of accident reports is to provide infor-   31.___
mation that may be used to reduce the possibility of similar
accidents.
The MOST valuable entry on the report for this purpose is the
    A. name of the victim
    B. injury sustained by the victim
    C. cause of the accident
    D. location of the accident

32. Fires in buildings are of such complexity that   32.___
    A. no plans or methods of attack can be formulated in
       advance
    B. no planned procedures can be relied on
    C. an appointed committee is necessary to direct fighting
       at the fire
    D. the problem must be considered in advance and methods
       of attack formulated

33. Of the following types of fires, a soda-acid fire
    extinguisher is NOT recommended for
    A. electric motor controls   B. waste paper
    C. waste rags   D. wood desks

    33.____

34. A foam-type fire extinguisher extinguishes fires by
    A. cooling only   B. drenching only
    C. smothering only   D. cooling and smothering

    34.____

35. If a keg of nails had on it the words *Net Weight 10 pounds*,
    it would mean that the
    A. keg weighed 10 pounds without the nails
    B. nails and the keg together weighed 10 pounds
    C. nails weighed 10 pounds without the keg
    D. weight of 10 pounds is approximate

    35.____

36. In deciding which items should be stored together, the
    one of the following factors which is usually of LEAST
    importance is
    A. activity   B. class   C. cost   D. size

    36.____

37. Of the following, the MOST effective way to teach a
    subordinate how to store an item is to
    A. do it yourself while explaining
    B. explain the procedure verbally
    C. have him do it while you criticize
    D. let him look at photographs of the operation

    37.____

38. If a cleaner is doing excellent work, then the PROPER
    action of the custodian is to
    A. give him preferential assignments as a reward
    B. tell the other cleaners what excellent work he is doing
    C. praise his work at the earliest opportunity
    D. do nothing since the man may become over-confident

    38.____

39. A cleaner does very good work, but he has trouble getting
    to work on time.
    To get the man to come on time, you should
    A. bring him up on charges to stop the lateness once
       and for all
    B. have him report directly to you every time he is late
    C. talk over the problem with him to find its cause and
       possible solution
    D. threaten to transfer him if he cannot get to work on
       time

    39.____

40. When the National flag is to be flown at half staff, it
    should ALWAYS be hoisted
    A. slowly to half staff
    B. slowly to the peak of staff and then lowered slowly
       to half staff
    C. briskly to the peak of staff and then lowered slowly
       to half staff
    D. briskly to the peak of staff and then lowered briskly
       to half staff

    40.____

KEY (CORRECT ANSWERS)

1. B	11. C	21. A	31. C
2. D	12. A	22. C	32. D
3. B	13. B	23. C	33. A
4. D	14. B	24. B	34. D
5. B	15. B	25. C	35. C
6. A	16. A	26. B	36. C
7. A	17. C	27. B	37. A
8. A	18. C	28. D	38. C
9. B	19. C	29. B	39. C
10. D	20. D	30. D	40. C

EXAMINATION SECTION
TEST 1

DIRECTIONS: Each question or incomplete statement is followed by several suggested answers or completions. Select the one that BEST answers the question or completes the statement. *PRINT THE LETTER OF THE CORRECT ANSWER IN THE SPACE AT THE RIGHT.*

1. The flow of oil in an automatic rotary cup oil burner is regulated by a(n)   1.____

    A. thermostat   B. metering valve
    C. pressure relief valve   D. electric eye

2. The type of fuel which must be *pre-heated* before it can be burned efficiently is   2.____

    A. natural gas   B. pea coal
    C. Number 2 oil   D. Number 6 oil

3. A suction gauge in a fuel-oil transfer system is *usually* located   3.____

    A. *before* the strainer
    B. *after* the strainer and *before* the pump
    C. *after* the pump and *before* the pressure relief valve
    D. *after* the pressure relief valve

4. The FIRST item that should be checked before starting the fire in a steam boiler is the   4.____

    A. thermostat   B. vacuum pump
    C. boiler water level   D. steam pressure

5. Operation of a boiler that has been *sealed* by the department of buildings is   5.____

    A. prohibited
    B. permitted when the outside temperature is below 32° F
    C. permitted between the hours of 6:00 A.M. and 8:00 A.M. and 9:00 P.M. and 11:00 P.M.
    D. permitted only for the purposes of heating domestic water

6. Lowering the thermostat setting by 5 degrees during the heating season will result in a fuel saving of, *most nearly,* _____ percent.   6.____

    A. 2   B. 5   C. 20   D. 50

7. An electrically-driven rotary fuel oil pump must be protected from internal damage by the installation in the oil line of a   7.____

    A. discharge-side strainer   B. check valve
    C. suction gauge   D. pressure relief valve

8. The air pollution code states that no person shall cause or permit the emission of an air contaminant of a density which appears as dark or darker than Number _____ on the standard smoke chart.   8.____

    A. One   B. Two
    C. Three   D. Four

9. When a glass globe is put back over a newly-replaced light bulb in a ceiling light fixture, the holding screws on the globe should be tightened, then loosened one half turn. This is done MAINLY to prevent

   A. fires caused by electrical short circuits
   B. cracking of the globe due to heat expansion
   C. falling of the globe from the light fixture
   D. building up of harmful gases inside the globe

9.___

10. Standard 120-volt plug-type fuses are *generally* rated in

   A. farads   B. ohms   C. watts   D. amperes

10.___

11. Standard 120-volt electric light bulbs are *generally* rated in

   A. farads   B. ohms   C. watts   D. amperes

11.___

12. A cleaner informs you that his electrical vacuum cleaner is not working even though he tried the off-on switch several times and checked to see that the plug was still in the wall outlet.
Of the following, the FIRST course of action you should take in this situation is to

   A. determine if the circuit-breaker has tripped out
   B. take apart the vacuum cleaner
   C. replace the electric cord on the vacuum cleaner
   D. replace the electrical outlet

12.___

13. The one of the following that is the MOST practical method for a building custodian to use in making a temporary repair in a straight portion of a water pipe which has a small leak is to

   A. attach a clamped patch over the leak
   B. weld or braze the pipe, depending on the material
   C. drill and tap the pipe, then insert a plug
   D. fill the hole with an epoxy sealer

13.___

14. The PRIMARY function of the packing which is generally found in the stuffing box of a centrifugal pump is to

   A. compensate for misalignment of the pump shaft
   B. prevent leakage of the fluid
   C. control the discharge rate of the pump
   D. provide support for the pump shaft

14.___

15. A pipe coupling is a plumbing fitting that is *most commonly* used to join

   A. two pieces of threaded pipe of the same diameter
   B. a large diameter tubing to a smaller diameter threaded pipe
   C. two pieces of threaded pipe of different diameters
   D. a large diameter threaded pipe to a smaller diameter tubing

15.___

16. Of the following, the MOST important reason for replacing a worn washer in a dripping faucet as soon as possible is to prevent   16._____

    A. overflow of the sink tap
    B. the mixture of hot and cold water in the sink
    C. damage to the faucet parts that can be the result of overtightening the stem
    D. air from entering the supply line

17. Window glass is secured mechanically in wood windows by   17._____

    A. glazing points   B. enamel paint
    C. screws   D. putty

18. In carpentry work, the *most commonly* used hand saw is the _____ saw.   18._____

    A. hack   B. rip   C. buck   D. cross-cut

19. The device which *usually* keeps a doorknob from rotating on the spindle is a   19._____

    A. cotter pin   B. tapered key
    C. set screw   D. stop screw

20. The *one* of the following types of nails that *usually* requires the use of a tool known as a nail set is the _____ nail.   20._____

    A. finishing   B. sheet rock   C. 6-penny   D. cut

21. The following tasks are frequently done when an office is cleaned: 21._____
        I. The floor is vacuumed.
        II. The ash trays and waste baskets are emptied.
        III. The desks and furniture are dusted.
The ORDER in which these tasks should *generally* be done is:

    A. I, II, III   B. II, III, I   C. III, II, I   D. I, III, II

22. When wax is applied to a floor by the use of a twine mop with handle, the wax should be _____ with the mop.   22._____

    A. applied in thin coats
    B. applied in heavy coats
    C. poured on the floor, then spread
    D. dropped on the floor, then spread

23. The BEST way to clean dust from an accoustical-type ceiling is with a   23._____

    A. strong soap solution   B. wet sponge
    C. vacuum cleaner   D. stream of water

24. Of the following, the MOST important reason why a wet mop should NOT be wrung out by hand is that   24._____

    A. the strings of the mop will be damaged by hand-wringing
    B. sharp objects picked up by the mop may injure the hands
    C. the mop cannot be made dry enough by hand-wringing
    D. fine dirt will become embedded in the strings of the mop

25. When a painted wall is washed by hand, the wall should be washed from the   25.___

    A. *top down,* with a soaking *wet* sponge
    B. *bottom up,* with a soaking *wet* sponge
    C. *top down,* with a *damp* sponge
    D. *bottom up,* with a *damp* sponge

26. When a painted wall is brushed with a clean lamb's wool duster, the duster should be   26.___
drawn _____ with a _____ pressure.

    A. *downward; light*
    B. *upward; light*
    C. *downward; firm*
    D. *upward; firm*

27. The *one* of the following terms which BEST describes the size of a floor brush is   27.___

    A. 72-cubic inch   B. 32-ounce
    C. 24-inch   D. 10-square foot

28. Terrazzo floors should be mopped periodically with a(n)   28.___

    A. acid solution
    B. neutral detergent in warm water
    C. mop treated with kerosene
    D. strong alkaline solution

29. The MAIN reason why the handle of a reversible floor brush should be shifted from one   29.___
side of the brush block to the opposite side is to

    A. change the angle at which the brush sweeps the floor
    B. give equal wear to both sides of the brush
    C. permit the brush to sweep hard-to-reach areas
    D. make it easier to sweep backward

30. When a long corridor is swept with a floor brush, it is *good* practice to   30.___

    A. push the brush with moderately long strokes and flick it after each stroke
    B. press on the brush and push it the whole length of the corridor in one sweep
    C. pull the brush inward with short, brisk strokes
    D. sweep across rather than down the length of the corridor

KEY (CORRECT ANSWERS)

1.	B		16.	C
2.	D		17.	A
3.	B		18.	D
4.	C		19.	C
5.	A		20.	A
6.	C		21.	B
7.	D		22.	A
8.	B		23.	C
9.	B		24.	B
10.	D		25.	D
11.	C		26.	A
12.	A		27.	C
13.	A		28.	B
14.	B		29.	B
15.	A		30.	A

———

TEST 2

DIRECTIONS: Each question or incomplete statement is followed by several suggested answers or completions. Select the one that BEST answers the question or completes the statement. *PRINT THE LETTER OF THE CORRECT ANSWER IN THE SPACE AT THE RIGHT.*

1. Of the following office cleaning jobs performed during the year, the *one* which should be done MOST frequently is

    1.___

    A. cleaning the fluorescent lights
    B. dusting the Venetian blinds
    C. cleaning the bookcase glass
    D. carpet-sweeping the rug

2. The BEST polishing agent to use on wood furniture is

    2.___

    A. pumice
    C. water emulsion wax
    B. paste wax
    D. neat's-foot oil

3. Lemon oil polish is used BEST to polish

    3.___

    A. exterior bronze
    C. leather seats
    B. marble walls
    D. lacquered metal

4. Cleaning with trisodium phosphate is *most likely* to damage

    4.___

    A. toilet bowls
    C. polished marble floors
    B. drain pipes
    D. rubber tile floors

5. Of the following cleaning agents, the one which should NOT be used to remove stains from urinals is

    5.___

    A. caustic lye
    C. oxalic acid
    B. detergent
    D. muriatic acid

6. The one of the following cleaners which *generally* contains an abrasive is

    6.___

    A. caustic lye
    C. scouring powder
    B. trisodium phosphate
    D. ammonia

7. The instructions on a box of cleaning powder say: *Mix one pound of cleaning powder in four gallons of water.* According to these instructions, how many ounces of cleaning powder should be mixed in one gallon of water?

    7.___

    A. 4   B. 8   C. 12   D. 16

8. In accordance with recommended practice, a dust mop, when not being used, should be stored

    8.___

    A. *hanging,* handle end down
    B. *hanging,* handle end up
    C. *standing* on the floor, handle end down
    D. *standing* on the floor, handle end up

9. The two types of floors found in public buildings are classified as *hard floors* and *soft floors.* 9.____
   An example of a *hard floor* is one made of

   A. linoleum   B. cork
   C. ceramic tile   D. asphalt tile

10. A squeegee is a tool that is MAINLY used to clean 10.____

    A. painted walls   B. radiator covers
    C. window glass   D. ceramic tile floors

11. The BEST way for a building custodian to determine whether a cleaner is doing his work well is by 11.____

    A. observing the cleaner at work for several hours
    B. asking the cleaner questions about the work
    C. asking other cleaners to rate his work
    D. inspecting the cleanliness of the spaces assigned to the cleaner

12. The PRIMARY purpose of using a disinfectant material is to 12.____

    A. kill germs   B. destroy odors
    C. remove stains   D. kill insects

13. Windows should be washed by using a solution of warm water mixed with 13.____

    A. chlorine bleach   B. kerosene
    C. ammonia   D. soft soap

14. Of the following, the MOST effective way to reduce waste of cleaning tools is to 14.____

    A. keep careful records of how often tools are issued
    B. require that the old tool be returned before issuing a new one
    C. require that all tools be used for a fixed number of hours before replacing them
    D. train the cleaners to use the tools properly

15. The number of square feet of unobstructed corridor floor space that a cleaner should sweep in an hour is, *most nearly,* 15.____

    A. 1200   B. 2400   C. 4000   D. 6000

16. Sweeping compound is used on concrete floors MAINLY to 16.____

    A. polish the floor
    B. keep the dust down
    C. soften the encrusted dirt
    D. provide a non-slip surface

17. The BEST attachment to use on an electric scrubbing machine when stripping waxed resilient flooring is a 17.____

    A. nylon disk   B. soft brush
    C. steel wool pad   D. pumice wheel

18. A counter brush is BEST suited to cleaning   18.___

    A. water cooler drains   B. radiators
    C. light fixtures   D. lavatory fixtures

19. Improper use of a carbon-dioxide type portable fire extinguisher may cause injury to the   19.___
operator because

    A. handling the nozzle during discharge can cause frostbite to the skin
    B. carbon dioxide is highly poisonous if breathed into the lungs
    C. use of carbon dioxide on an oil fire can cause a chemical explosion
    D. the powdery residue left by the discharge is highly caustic to the skin

20. When using a portable single ladder with ten rungs, the GREATEST number of rungs   20.___
that a cleaner should climb up is

    A. 7   B. 8   C. 9   D. 10

21. Of the following types of portable fire extinguishers, the one which should be used to   21.___
control a fire in or around live electrical equipment is the _____ type.

    A. foam   B. soda-acid
    C. carbon-dioxide   D. gas-cartridge water

22. The MOST frequent cause of accidental injuries to workers on the job is   22.___

    A. unsafe working practices of employees
    B. poor design of buildings and working areas
    C. lack of warning signs in hazardous working areas
    D. lack of adequate safety guards on equipment and machinery

23. Of the following, the MOST important purpose of preparing an accident report on an   23.___
injury to a cleaner is to help

    A. collect statistics on different types of accidents
    B. calm the feelings of the injured cleaner
    C. prevent similar accidents in the future
    D. prove that the cleaner was at fault

24. The one of the following types of locks that is used on emergency exit doors is the   24.___
_____ bolt.

    A. panic   B. dead   C. cinch   D. toggle

25. The one of the following types of locks that *usually* contains both a live bolt and a dead   25.___
bolt is a _____ lock.

    A. mortise   B. double-hung window
    C. loose pin butt   D. window frame

KEY (CORRECT ANSWERS)

1.	D	11.	D
2.	B	12.	A
3.	A	13.	C
4.	C	14.	D
5.	D	15.	D
6.	C	16.	B
7.	A	17.	A
8.	B	18.	B
9.	C	19.	A
10.	C	20.	B

21.	C
22.	A
23.	C
24.	A
25.	A

———

EXAMINATION SECTION
TEST 1

DIRECTIONS: Each question or incomplete statement is followed by several suggested
answers or completions. Select the one that BEST answers the question or
completes the statement. *PRINT THE LETTER OF THE CORRECT ANSWER
IN THE SPACE AT THE RIGHT.*

1.   Linseed oil is MOST commonly used to   1._____

   A.   seal wooden floors
   B.   polish brass fixtures
   C.   thin exterior oil base paints
   D.   lubricate fan bearings

2.   The APPROXIMATE number of square feet of unobstructed corridor floorspace that one   2._____
cleaner can sweep in an hour is

   A.   1200   B.   2400   C.   4000   D.   6000

3.   Of the following materials, the one MOST effective in dusting office furniture is a   3._____

   A.   silk cloth   B.   chamois
   C.   soft cotton cloth   D.   counter brush

4.   Of the following materials, the one that should be used to produce the MOST resilient   4._____
flooring is

   A.   concrete   B.   terrazzo
   C.   ceramic tile   D.   asphalt tile

5.   Sweeping compound is used on concrete floors MAINLY to   5._____

   A.   keep the dust down
   B.   polish the floor
   C.   harden the floor surface
   D.   indicate which part of the floor has not been swept

6.   The type of floor finish or wax that will produce an anti-slip surface on resilient floor cov-   6._____
erings is

   A.   resin-based floor finish
   B.   water emulsion wax
   C.   paste wax
   D.   paraffin

7.   High sheen and good wearing qualities can be obtained when polishing a waxed floor by   7._____
using an electric scrubbing machine equipped with

   A.   nylon disks   B.   soft brushes
   C.   steel wool pads   D.   pumice wheels

8.   Spalling of the surface of a marble floor may result if the floor is washed with   8._____

   A.   a solution of trisodium phosphate   B.   a soft soap solution
   C.   a neutral liquid detergent solution D.   cold water

9. When not in use, a broom should be stored   9.___

    A. resting on the floor with the handle end down
    B. resting on the floor with the bristle end down
    C. hanging by the handle from a hook
    D. lying flat on the floor

10. The one of the following items which ordinarily requires the MOST time to wash is a(n)   10.___

    A. 5 ft x 10 ft Venetian blind
    B. 4 ft fluorescent fixture
    C. incandescent fixture
    D. 5 ft x 10 ft ceramic tile floor

11. A broom that has been properly used should GENERALLY be replaced after   11.___

    A. it has been used for one month
    B. its bristles have been worn down by more than one-third of their original length
    C. it has been used for two months
    D. its bristles have been worn down by more than two-thirds of their original length

12. The floor area of a room which measures 10 ft long x 10 ft wide is _____ sq. ft.   12.___

    A. 20   B. 40   C. 100   D. 1000

13. The FIRST thing that should be checked before an oil-fired, low-pressure steam boiler is started up in the morning is the   13.___

    A. boiler water level   B. stack temperature
    C. aquastat   D. vaporstat

14. The MAIN reason for preheating number 6 fuel oil before allowing it to enter an oil burner is to   14.___

    A. increase its viscosity
    B. decrease its viscosity
    C. increase its heating value
    D. decrease its flash point

15. A house pump is used to   15.___

    A. drain basements that become flooded
    B. pump sewage from the basement to the sewer
    C. pump city water to a roof storage tank
    D. circulate domestic hot water

16. The device which shuts down an automatic rotary cup oil burner when the steam pressure reaches a preset high limit is a   16.___

    A. pressure gage   B. pressurtrol
    C. safety valve   D. low water cutoff

17. A pressure gage connected to a compressed air tank USUALLY reads in   17.____

    A. pounds   B. pounds per square inch
    C. inches of mercury   D. feet of water

18. The device which shuts off the oil burner when the water level in the boiler is too low is   18.____
the

    A. feedwater regulator   B. low water cutoff
    C. high water alarm   D. programmer

19. The device which shuts down an oil burner when there is a flame failure is the   19.____

    A. stack switch   B. thermostat
    C. manometer   D. modutrol motor

20. The switch which is used to shut off the oil burner in case of a fire in the boiler room is   20.____
located

    A. on the programmer cover
    B. near the boiler room entrance
    C. on the burner motor
    D. in the custodian's office

21. The MOST likely reason for a cold water faucet to continue to drip after its washer has   21.____
been replaced is a defective

    A. handle   B. stem   C. seat   D. bib

22. In water lines, the type of valve which should always be either fully open or fully closed is   22.____
the

    A. needle valve   B. gate valve
    C. globe valve   D. mixing valve

23. The BEST tool to use on a 1" galvanized iron pipe nipple when unscrewing the nipple   23.____
from a coupling is a _____ wrench.

    A. crescent   B. stillson   C. monkey   D. spud

24. The BEST way to locate a leak in a natural gas pipe line is to   24.____

    A. hold a lighted match under the pipe and move it along the length of the pipe slowly
    B. hold a lighted match about two inches above the pipe and move it along the length
       of the pipe slowly
    C. coat the pipe with a soapy solution and watch for bubbles
    D. shut off the gas at the meter and then coat the pipe with a soapy solution and
       watch for bubbles

25. When comparing a 60 watt yellow bulb with a 60 watt clear bulb, it can be said that they   25.____
BOTH

    A. give the same amount of light
    B. use the same amount of power
    C. will burn for at least 60 hours
    D. will burn for at least 60 days

26. The output capacity of an electric motor is USUALLY rated in 26.____

    A. kilowatts
    B. horsepower
    C. percent
    D. cubic feet

27. A fuse will burn out whenever it is subjected to excessive 27.____

    A. resistance
    B. voltage
    C. current
    D. capacitance

28. Of the following, the device which uses the GREATEST amount of electric power is the 28.____

    A. electric typewriter
    B. $\frac{1}{4}$ inch electric drill
    C. floor scrubbing machine
    D. oil burner ignition transformer

29. Meters which indicate the electric power consumed in a public building are read in 29.____

    A. kilowatt-hours
    B. volts
    C. cubic feet
    D. degree days

30. Tongue and groove lumber is used for 30.____

    A. desk drawers
    B. hardwood floors
    C. picture frames
    D. cabinet doors

31. When hand sawing a 1" x 4" board parallel to the grain of the wood, the BEST saw to use 31.____
    is the _____ saw.

    A. cross-cut
    B. back
    C. hack
    D. rip

32. The BEST tool to use to make a recess for the head of a flat-head wood screw is a(n) 32.____

    A. counterbore
    B. countersink
    C. auger
    D. nail set

33. In attaching two pieces of wood with a nut and bolt, the holes drilled should be 33.____

    A. slightly undersize in one piece, slightly oversize in the other
    B. slightly oversize in both pieces
    C. slightly undersize in both pieces
    D. drilled from opposite sides of the joint

34. The one of the following transmission devices which should be oiled MOST often is the 34.____

    A. V-belt
    B. roller chain
    C. rigid coupling
    D. clutch plate

35. A motor-generator set is USUALLY part of a(n) 35.____

    A. steam boiler
    B. hydraulic elevator
    C. electric elevator
    D. incinerator

36. The one of the following devices which MOST frequently contains hydraulic fluid is a   36.____

    A. door closer   B. worm gear reducer
    C. foam fire extinguisher   D. hand winch

37. A breakdown of the causes of accidental injuries by percent would show that such inju-   37.____
ries are *most nearly* caused

    A. 100 percent by unsafe physical working conditions
    B. 100 percent by unsafe acts of people
    C. 50 percent by unsafe physical working conditions and 50 percent by unsafe acts of people
    D. 20 percent by unsafe physical working conditions and 80 percent by unsafe acts of people

38. When using an eight-foot stepladder, a worker should climb up not more than _____   38.____
rungs.

    A. 4   B. 5   C. 6   D. 7

39. A supervisor interested in the safety of his subordinates would NOT permit   39.____

    A. using a wooden rule to take measurements near electrical apparatus
    B. using a machinist's hammer to strike a chisel
    C. removing metal chips from a machine with a rag
    D. testing the heat of a soldering iron with a piece of solder

40. If a worker feels an electric shock while using a portable electric drill, he should immedi-   40.____
ately

    A. stand on a piece of scrap lumber
    B. reverse the plug in the receptacle
    C. hold onto a grounded pipe or piece of metal
    D. take the drill out of service

KEY (CORRECT ANSWERS)

1.	C	11.	B	21.	C	31.	D
2.	D	12.	C	22.	B	32.	B
3.	C	13.	A	23.	B	33.	B
4.	D	14.	A	24.	C	34.	B
5.	A	15.	C	25.	B	35.	C
6.	A	16.	B	26.	B	36.	A
7.	B	17.	B	27.	C	37.	D
8.	A	18.	B	28.	C	38.	C
9.	C	19.	A	29.	A	39.	C
10.	A	20.	B	30.	B	40.	D

TEST 2

DIRECTIONS: Each question or incomplete statement is followed by several suggested answers or completions. Select the one that BEST answers the question or completes the statement. *PRINT THE LETTER OF THE CORRECT ANSWER IN THE SPACE AT THE RIGHT.*

1. During a shortage of custodial help in a public building, the cleaning task which will probably receive LEAST attention is

    A. picking up sweepings   B. emptying ashtrays
    C. washing walls   D. dust-mopping offices

1.___

2. Of the following substances commonly used on floors, the MOST flammable is

    A. resin-based floor finish
    B. floor sealer
    C. water emulsion wax
    D. trisodium phosphate

2.___

3. The MOST effective method for cleaning badly soiled carpeting is

    A. wet shampooing   B. vacuum cleaning
    C. dry shampooing   D. wire brushing

3.___

4. Before repainting becomes necessary, a painted wall can USUALLY be washed completely

    A. only once   B. two or three times
    C. eight to ten times   D. sixteen to twenty times

4.___

5. The FIRST step in routine cleaning of offices at night should be

    A. sweeping floors   B. emptying ashtrays
    C. dusting furniture   D. damp mopping the floors

5.___

6. Among the factors pertaining to the maintenance and cleaning of a building, the one MOST likely to be under the control of the building custodian is the

    A. size of the area   B. density of occupancy
    C. type of occupancy   D. standards to be maintained

6.___

7. "Treated" or "dustless" sweeping of resilient-type floors requires

    A. spraying the floors with water to keep the dust down
    B. spreading sweeping compound on the floor
    C. sweeping cloths that are chemically treated with mineral oil
    D. spraying the sweeping tool with neatsfoot oil

7.___

8. A modern central vacuum cleaner system

    A. is cheaper to operate than one portable machine
    B. generally produces less suction than a portable machine
    C. conveys the dirt directly to a basement tank
    D. must be operated only in the daytime

8.___

9. Oxalic acid can be used to   9._____

    A. remove ink spots from wood
    B. clear floor drains
    C. solder copper flashing
    D. polish brass

10. The BEST material for sealing a terrazzo floor is   10._____

    A. varnish   B. a penetrating seal
    C. shellac   D. a surface seal

11. The MOST troublesome feature in cleaning public washrooms is   11._____

    A. cleaning and deodorizing the urinals
    B. washing the toilet bowls
    C. mopping the tile floors
    D. removing chewing gum from the floors

12. In order to improve its appearance, extend its life, and reduce the labor involved in dust-   12._____
ing, wood furniture should be polished with

    A. an oil polish
    B. a water emulsion wax
    C. a silicone and spirit chemical spray
    D. clear water

13. Ringelmann charts are useful in determining   13._____

    A. interest rates
    B. smoke density
    C. standard times for cleaning operations
    D. fuel consumption

14. A fusible plug is USUALLY found in a   14._____

    A. lighting panel   B. fire door
    C. boiler wall   D. house tank

15. In an air conditioned office, MOST people would feel comfortable when the room temper-   15._____
ature and humidity are maintained, respectively, at

    A. 75° F and 50%   B. 70° F and 30%
    C. 75° F and 20%   D. 65° F and 75%

16. The one of the following sets of conditions which will provide the MOST efficient combus-   16._____
tion in an oil-fired low-temperature steam boiler is _____ stack temperature, _____
CO_2.

    A. 400° F, 12%   B. 500° F, 10%
    C. 600° F, 8%   D. 700° F, 6%

17. The BEST way for a building custodian to tell if the night cleaners have done their work well is to check   17.___

    A. on how much cleaning material has been used
    B. on how much waste paper was collected
    C. the building for cleanliness
    D. the floor mops to see if they are still wet

18. The one of the following which is the BEST reason for introducing a training program is that the   18.___

    A. quality of work is above standard
    B. employees are all experienced
    C. accident rate is too high
    D. tenant complaints are negligible

19. The FIRST step in training an inexperienced individual in a particular job is to   19.___

    A. put him to work and watch for mistakes
    B. put him to work and tell him to call for help if he needs it
    C. put him at ease and then find out what he knows about the work
    D. tell him to watch the least experienced worker on the job because the training is still fresh in his mind

20. As used in job analysis, the term "job breakdown" means   20.___

    A. any equipment failure
    B. any failure on the part of the worker to complete the job
    C. dividing the job into a series of steps
    D. reducing the number of workers by 50 percent

21. At times when a public building is closed to the public, the building custodian should   21.___

    A. keep all doors locked and admit no one
    B. admit only custodial employees
    C. admit anyone as long as he signs the log
    D. admit only those who have business in the building

22. When a public building is equipped for security purposes with exterior lights on or around the building, the lights should be kept lit   22.___

    A. all night except for Saturdays, Sundays, and holidays
    B. twenty-four hours a day on weekends
    C. throughout the night, every night of the week
    D. until midnight, every night of the week

23. Custodial workers are MOST liable to injury when they are engaged in   23.___

    A. sweeping floors   B. mopping floors
    C. dusting furniture   D. moving furniture

24. The BEST place to store a wooden stepladder is   24.____

     A. in a boiler room
     B. in a stairwell
     C. in a dry room
     D. outside a basement window provided that there is a locked grating overhead

25. Of the following, the BEST action for a building custodian to take when he notices that an   25.____
office worker in his building has a hot plate connected to a heavily loaded electric circuit
is to

     A. remove the hot plate from the office when its owner is not present
     B. demand that the office worker remove the hot plate immediately
     C. write a report to the supervisor of the office requesting corrective action
     D. ignore the situation

26. In dealing with the public, a building custodian should be   26.____

     A. indulgent   B. courteous
     C. disagreeable   D. unavailable

27. If a building custodian sees a group of people in front of his building preparing to form a   27.____
picket line, he should

     A. turn on a lawn sprinkler to spray the pickets
     B. order the pickets off the sidewalk in front of the building
     C. show the pickets he is sympathetic with their complaint
     D. contact his supervisor immediately for instructions

28. When electric service in a public building is to be shut off from 10 A.M. Tuesday to 11:30   28.____
the next morning because a new electric feeder cable is being installed, the building custodian should

     A. prepare a memo to all office supervisors in the building, notifying them of the situa-
tion, and deliver a copy to each office as soon as possible
     B. prepare a notice of the impending power stoppage and post it in the lobby early
Tuesday morning
     C. tell the electrical contractor to notify the tenants when he is about to shut off the
power
     D. discontinue elevator service at 10 A.M. on Tuesday as an indication to the tenants
that the power supply is off

29. The BEST way to remove some small pieces of broken glass from a floor is to   29.____

     A. use a brush and dustpan
     B. pick up the pieces carefully with your hands
     C. use a wet mop and a wringer
     D. sweep the pieces into the corner of the room

30. There is a two-light fixture in the room where you are working. One of the light bulbs goes   30.____
out, and you need more light to work by. You should

     A. change the fuse in the fuse box
     B. have a new bulb put in
     C. call for an electrician and stop work till he comes
     D. find out what is causing the short circuit

31. While working on the job, you accidently break a window pane. No one is around, and you are able to clean up the broken pieces of glass. It would then be BEST for you to
31.___

    A. leave a note near the window that a new glass has to be put in because it was accidently broken
    B. forget about the whole thing because the window was not broken on purpose
    C. write a report to your supervisor telling him that you saw a broken window pane that has to be fixed
    D. tell your supervisor that you accidently broke the window pane while working

32. Many machines have certain safety devices for the operators. The MOST important reason for having these safety devices is to
32.___

    A. increase the amount of work that the machines can do
    B. permit repairs to be made on the machines without shutting them down
    C. help prevent accidents to people who use the machines
    D. reduce the cost of electric power needed to run the machines

Questions 33-36.

DIRECTIONS: Answer Questions 33 through 36 only according to the information given in the following passage.

MOPPING FLOORS

When mopping hardened cement floors, either painted or unpainted, a soap and water mixture should be used. This should be made by dissolving 1/2 a cup of soft soap in a pail of hot water. It is not desirable, however, under any circumstances, to use a soap and water mixture on cement floors that are not hardened. For mopping this type of floor, it is recommended that the cleaning agent be made up of 2 ounces of laundry soda mixed in a pail of water.

Soaps are not generally used on hard tile floors because slippery films may build up on the floor. It is generally recommended that these floors be mopped using a pail of hot water in which has been mixed 2 ounces of washing powder for each gallon of water. The floors should then be rinsed thoroughly.

After the mopping is finished, proper care should be taken of the mop. This is done by first cleaning the mop in clear warm water. Then it should be wrung out, after which the strands of the mop should be untangled. Finally, the mop should be hung by its handle to dry.

33. According to the above passage, you should NEVER use a soap and water mixture when mopping _____ floors.
33.___

    A. hardened cement   B. painted
    C. unhardened cement   D. unpainted

34. According to the above passage, using laundry soda mixed in a pail of water as a cleaning agent is recommended for
34.___

    A. all floors
    B. all floors except hard tile floors
    C. some cement floors
    D. linoleum floor coverings only

35. According to the above passage, the GENERALLY recommended mixture for mopping hard tile floors is   35.____

    A. 1/2 cup of soft soap for each gallon of hot water
    B. 1/2 cup of soft soap in a pail of hot water
    C. 2 ounces of washing powder in a pail of hot water
    D. 2 ounches of washing powder for each gallon of hot water

36. According to the above passage, the PROPER care of a mop after it is used includes   36.____

    A. cleaning it in clear cold water and hanging it by its handle to dry
    B. wringing it out, untangling, and drying it
    C. untangling its strands before wringing it out
    D. untangling its strands while cleaning it in clear water

Questions 37-40.

DIRECTIONS: Answer Questions 37 through 40 only according to the information given in the following passage.

ACCIDENT PREVENTION

Many accidents and injuries can be prevented if employees learn to be move careful. The wearing of shoes with thin or badly worn soles or open toes can easily lead to foot injuries from tacks, nails, and chair and desk legs. Loose or torn clothing should not be worn near moving machinery. This is especially true of neckties which can very easily become caught in the machine. You should not place objects so that they block or partly block hallways, corridors, or other passageways. Even when they are stored in the proper place, tools, supplies, and equipment should be carefully placed or piled so as not to fall, nor have anything stick out from a pile. Before cabinets, lockers or ladders are moved, the tops should be cleared of anything which might injure someone or fall off. If necessary, use a dolly to move these or other bulky objects.

Despite all efforts to avoid accidents and injuries, however, some will happen. If an employee is injured, no matter how small the injury, he should report it to his supervisor and have the injury treated. A small cut that is not attended to can easily become infected and can cause more trouble than some injuries which at first seem more serious. It never pays to take chances.

37. According to the above passage, the one statement that is NOT true is that   37.____

    A. by being more careful, employees can reduce the number of accidents that happen
    B. women should wear shoes with open toes for comfort when working
    C. supplies should be piled so that nothing is sticking out from the pile
    D. if an employee sprains his wrist at work, he should tell his supervisor about it

38. According to the above passage, you should NOT wear loose clothing when you are   38.____

    A. in a corridor
    B. storing tools
    C. opening cabinets
    D. near moving machinery

39. According to the above passage, before moving a ladder, you should

    A. test all the rungs
    B. get a dolly to carry the ladder at all times
    C. remove everything from the top of the ladder which might fall off
    D. remove your necktie

39.___

40. According to the above passage, an employee who gets a slight cut should

    A. have it treated to help prevent infection
    B. know that a slight cut becomes more easily infected than a big cut
    C. pay no attention to it as it can't become serious
    D. realize that it is more serious than any other type of injury

40.___

_____

KEY (CORRECT ANSWERS)

1.	C	11.	A	21.	D	31.	D
2.	B	12.	C	22.	C	32.	C
3.	A	13.	B	23.	D	33.	C
4.	B	14.	C	24.	C	34.	C
5.	B	15.	A	25.	C	35.	D
6.	D	16.	A	26.	B	36.	B
7.	C	17.	C	27.	D	37.	B
8.	C	18.	C	28.	A	38.	D
9.	A	19.	C	29.	A	39.	C
10.	B	20.	C	30.	B	40.	A

_____

TEST 3

DIRECTIONS: Each question or incomplete statement is followed by several suggested answers or completions. Select the one that BEST answers the question or completes the statement. *PRINT THE LETTER OF THE CORRECT ANSWER IN THE SPACE AT THE RIGHT.*

1. An electric motor fire should be put out with an extinguisher that uses   1.____
   A. carbon dioxide   B. soda-acid
   C. foam   D. a pump tank

2. The charge in a soda-acid fire extinguisher should be replaced once   2.____
   A. a month   B. every three months
   C. every six months   D. a year

3. An elevator machinery room should have a fire extinguisher of the _____ type. 3.____
   A. soda-acid   B. foam
   C. carbon dioxide   D. sand pail

4. The national flag should be raised   4.____
   A. slowly and lowered briskly
   B. briskly and lowered slowly
   C. briskly and lowered briskly
   D. slowly and lowered slowly

5. The material which is used to seal the outside edges of a pane of window glass is 5.____
   A. stellite   B. putty
   C. plastic wood   D. caulking compound

6. The ceiling of a room which measures 20 ft x 30 ft is to be given two coats of paint. If one 6.____
   gallon of paint will cover 500 square feet, the two coats of paint will require a MINIMUM
   of _____ gallons.
   A. 1.5   B. 2   C. 2.4   D. 3.2

7. Rubbish, sticks, and papers on the lawn in front of a building should be collected by using 7.____
   a
   A. rake   B. broom
   C. paper sticker   D. hoe

8. Mortar stains on brickwork can be scrubbed off by using a solution of   8.____
   A. benzine   B. tri-sodium phosphate
   C. muriatic acid   D. acetic acid

9. The BEST chemical for melting ice on sidewalks is   9.____
   A. sodium chloride   B. calcium carbonate
   C. hydrogen sulphide   D. calcium chloride

10. Before painting a kitchen wall, 10.___

    A. a degreaser must be mixed with the paint
    B. all traces of grease must be washed off
    C. a water-base paint must be used to dissolve the grease
    D. the walls must be sanded to remove all traces of grease and old paint

11. For interior walls which must be washed very often, the PREFERRED paint is 11.___

    A. enamel   B. flat
    C. exterior varnish   D. calsomine

12. A type of window which is USUALLY equipped with sash cords or chains is the _____ type. 12.___

    A. hopper   B. awning
    C. casement   D. double-hung

13. The slats of a Venetian blind are usually tilted by a device containing a _____ gear. 13.___

    A. worm   B. spur   C. hypoid   D. bevil

14. When washing the outside of a window with a narrow inside sill, a window cleaner should place his water pail on 14.___

    A. the outside window sill
    B. the nearest desk or chair
    C. a radiator at the center of the window
    D. the floor at a convenient point toward one side of the window

15. In order to determine the carrying capacity of a passenger elevator, a custodian would have to 15.___

    A. measure the floor area
    B. check the diameter of the cable
    C. read the inspection certificate
    D. read the motor nameplate

16. Before pruning a tree, the FIRST step should be to determine 16.___

    A. if there is insect infestation
    B. the general health of the tree
    C. the desired results
    D. amount of excess foliage

17. Tree fertilizer should have a high content of 17.___

    A. slaked lime   B. chlordane
    C. rose dust   D. nitrogen

18. A gasoline-driven snow blower should be stored for the summer with its fuel tank 18.___

    A. filled with gasoline
    B. and fuel lines drained
    C. filled with water
    D. half filled with number 4 fuel oil

19. A pipe that "sweats" in the summer time PROBABLY contains 19.____

    A. hot water   B. low pressure steam
    C. domestic gas   D. cold water

20. A good preventive maintenance program requires that each item of equipment be 20.____

    A. represented by an up-to-date record card on file
    B. lubricated daily
    C. brand new at the start of the program
    D. painted inside and out

Questions 21-24.

DIRECTIONS: Questions 21 through 24, inclusive, are to be answered SOLELY on the basis of the following paragraph.

All cleaning agents and supplies should be kept in a central storeroom which should be kept looked and only the custodian, storekeeper and foreman should have keys. Shelving should be provided for the smaller items, while barrels containing scouring powder or other bulk material should be set on the floor or on special cradles. Each compartment in the shelves should be marked plainly and only the item indicated stored therein. Each barrel should also be marked plainly. It may also be desirable to keep special items such as electric lamps, flashlight batteries, etc., in a locked cabinet or separate room to which only the custodian and the night building foreman have keys.

21. According to the above paragraph, scouring powder 21.____

    A. should be kept on shelves
    B. comes in one-pound cans
    C. should be kept in a locked cabinet
    D. is a bulk material

22. According to the above paragraph, 22.____

    A. the storekeeper should not be entrusted with the safekeeping of light bulbs
    B. flashlight batteries should be stored in barrels
    C. the central storeroom should be kept locked
    D. only special items should be stored under lock and key

23. According to the above paragraph, 23.____

    A. each shelf compartment should contain at least four different items
    B. barrels must be stored in cradles
    C. all items stored should be in marked compartments
    D. crates of light bulbs should be stored in cradles

24. As used in the above paragraph, the word *cradle* means a 24.____

    A. dolly   B. support
    C. doll's bed   D. hand truck

Questions 25-28.

DIRECTIONS: Questions 25 through 28, inclusive, are to be answered SOLELY on the basis
of the following paragraph.

*There are on the market many cleaning agents for which amazing claims are made.
Chemical analysis shows that the majority of them are well-known chemicals slightly modified
and packaged and sold under various trade names. For that reason, the agents which have
been selected for your use are those whose cleaning properties are well-known and whose
use can be standardized. It is obviously undesirable to offer too wide a selection as that
would be confusing to the cleaner, but a sufficient number must be provided so that a satisfactory agent is available for each task.*

25.   According to the above paragraph,   25.____

    A.   there are few cleaning agents on the market
    B.   there are no really good cleaning agents on the market
    C.   cleaning agents are sold under several different brand names
    D.   all cleaning agents are the same

26.   According to the above paragraph,   26.____

    A.   all cleaning agents should be chemically analyzed before use
    B.   the best cleaning agents are those for which no claims are made by the manufac-
turer
    C.   different cleaning agents may be needed for different tasks
    D.   all cleaning agents have been standardized by the federal government

27.   As used in the above paragraph, the word *amazing* means   27.____

    A.   illegal   B.   untrue
    C.   astonishing   D.   specific

28.   As used in the above paragraph, the word *modified* means   28.____

    A.   changed   B.   refined   C.   labelled   D.   diluted

29.   The MAIN reason for keeping an inventory of housekeeping supplies is to   29.____

    A.   be sure that supplies are available when needed
    B.   determine the cost of the supplies
    C.   automatically prevent waste of the supplies
    D.   be sure that at least two years' supplies are on hand at all times

30.   Current daily records are MOST desirable in dealing with problems concerning   30.____

    A.   accidents
    B.   vandalism
    C.   employee time and attendance
    D.   the consumption of electricity

31.   The continuous record of activities taking place in a boiler room is called a   31.____

    A.   computer   B.   data bank
    C.   log book   D.   time sheet

32. The one of the following subjects of a fire prevention training program which is MOST readily applied on the job is the

    A. elimination of fire hazards
    B. use of portable fire extinguishers
    C. knowledge of types of fires
    D. method of reporting fires

32.____

33. A good supervisor will NOT

    A. tell his men what their jobs are and why they are important
    B. show his men how their jobs are to be done in the right way
    C. require some of the men to do their jobs in the presence of the supervisor demonstrating that they understand the job
    D. leave his men alone because they will always do their jobs correctly once they have received their instructions

33.____

34. When a supervisor sees a worker doing his job incorrectly, he should

    A. tell the worker to be more careful
    B. suspend the worker until he learns to do the job correctly
    C. tell the worker specifically how the job should be done
    D. scold the man

34.____

35. An office worker complains to a custodian that one of the cleaners broke off a branch of a plant which she kept on her desk and that she can identify the cleaner.
The BEST thing for the custodian to do is to

    A. convince her that the plant will grow another branch eventually
    B. make the cleaner apologize and pay for a new plant out of his own pocket
    C. sympathize with the office worker and assure her that he will speak to the cleaner about it
    D. tell her not to bother him about her personal property

35.____

36. An employee who is a good worker but is often late for work

    A. is lazy and should be dismissed
    B. cannot tell time
    C. can have no excuse for being late more than once a month
    D. should be questioned by his supervisor to try to find out why he is late

36.____

37. When starting any disciplinary action, a good supervisor should

    A. show his annoyance by losing his temper
    B. be apologetic
    C. be sarcastic
    D. be firm and positive

37.____

38. Good public relations can be damaged by a custodian who treats tenants, fellow workers, friends, relatives, and the public with

    A. courtesy
    B. consideration
    C. contempt
    D. respect

38.____

39. The BEST way for a supervisor to maintain good employee morale is to 39.___

    A. avoid praising any one employee
    B. always have an alibi for his own mistakes
    C. encourage cliques by given them information before giving it to other workers
    D. give adequate credit and praise when due

40. When a new employee reports to a custodian on his first day on the job, the custodian should 40.___

    A. extend a hearty welcome and make the new employee feel welcome
    B. have the man sit and wait for a while before seeing him so that the employee realizes how busy the custodian is
    C. warn him of stern disciplinary action if he is late or absent excessively
    D. tell him he probably will have difficulty doing the work so that he doesn't become overconfident

_____

KEY (CORRECT ANSWERS)

1. A	11. A	21. D	31. C
2. D	12. D	22. C	32. A
3. C	13. A	23. C	33. D
4. B	14. D	24. B	34. C
5. B	15. C	25. C	35. C
6. C	16. C	26. C	36. D
7. A	17. D	27. C	37. D
8. C	18. B	28. A	38. C
9. D	19. D	29. A	39. D
10. B	20. A	30. C	40. A

_____

EXAMINATION SECTION
TEST 1

DIRECTIONS: Each question or incomplete statement is followed by several suggested answers or completions. Select the one that BEST answers the question or completes the statement. *PRINT THE LETTER OF THE CORRECT ANSWER IN THE SPACE AT THE RIGHT.*

1. Of the following, the FIRST thing a custodian should do when he enters the boiler room to check on the operation of the boiler is to   1.____

   A. check the boiler water level
   B. blow down the boiler
   C. check the boiler water temperature
   D. check the fuel supply

2. Cleaners will usually be motivated to do a GOOD job by a custodian who   2.____

   A. lets them get away with poor performance
   B. treats them fairly
   C. treats some of them more favorably than others
   D. lets them take a nap in the afternoon

3. The MOST important aim of a training program in fire prevention is to train the custodial staff to   3.____

   A. be constantly alert to fire hazards
   B. assist the city fire department in extinguishing fires
   C. maintain the sprinkler system
   D. climb ladders safely

4. The one of the following which is NOT recommended for prolonging the useful life of a hair broom is to   4.____

   A. rotate the brush to avoid wear on one side only
   B. wash the brush by using it as a mop once a week
   C. comb the brush weekly
   D. hang the brush in storage to avoid resting on the bristles

5. A GOOD indication of the quality of the cleaning operation in a building is the   5.____

   A. amount of cleaning material used each month
   B. number of cleaners employed
   C. number of complaints of unsanitary conditions received
   D. number of square feet of hall space cleaned daily

6. Spontaneous ignition is MOST likely to occur in a   6.____

   A. pile of oily rags
   B. vented fuel oil tank
   C. metal file cabinet filled with papers in file folders
   D. covered metal container containing clean rags

7. A boiler test kit is used to test   7.____

    A. boiler water   B. fuel oil
    C. pressure gauges   D. steam consumption

8. The MOST common cause of a dripping faucet is a   8.____

    A. broken stem
    B. cracked bonnet
    C. worn washer
    D. loose retaining screw on the handle

9. The lighting systems in public buildings usually operate MOST NEARLY on _____ volts.   9.____

    A. 6   B. 24   C. 115   D. 220

10. A type of hammer which can be used to remove nails from wood is the   10.____

    A. ball-peen   B. mallet   C. sledge   D. claw

11. A vacuum pump is used in a(n) _____ heating system.   11.____

    A. steam   B. hot air
    C. hot water   D. electric

12. An expansion tank is used in a(n) heating system.   12.____

    A. steam   B. hot air
    C. hot water   D. electric

13. The thermostat in the office area of a public building should have a winter daytime setting   13.____
of about _____ ° F.

    A. 50   B. 60   C. 70   D. 80

14. The fuel oil which USUALLY requires preheating before it enters an oil burner is known   14.____
as

    A. #1   B. #2   C. #4   D. #6

15. The domestic hot water in a large public building is circulated by   15.____

    A. gravity flow
    B. a pump which runs continuously
    C. a pump which is controlled by water pressure
    D. a pump which is controlled by water temperature

16. The vaporstat on a rotary-cup boil burner senses   16.____

    A. oil temperature   B. primary air pressure
    C. secondary air pressure   D. oil pressure

17. The emergency switch for a fully automatic oil burner is USUALLY located   17.____

    A. at the entrance to the boiler room
    B. on the burner
    C. at the electrical distribution panel in the boiler room
    D. at the electric service meter panel

18. The try-cocks on a steam boiler are used to   18._____

    A. drain the boiler
    B. check the operation of the safety valves
    C. check the water level in the boiler
    D. drain the pressure gauge

19. The draft in a natural draft furnace is USUALLY measured in   19._____

    A. pounds   B. inches of mercury
    C. inches of water   D. cubic feet

20. The stack temperature in a low pressure oil-fired steam boiler installation should be   20._____
about _____ ° F.

    A. 212   B. 275   C. 350   D. 875

21. A material that transmits heat VERY POORLY is a good   21._____

    A. insulator   B. conductor
    C. radiator   D. convector

22. The asbestos covering on steam lines   22._____

    A. increases the flow of steam
    B. reduces the loss of heat
    C. increases the loss of heat
    D. prevents leaks

23. The air in a closed room that is heated by a radiator USUALLY   23._____

    A. settles to the floor   B. rises
    C. remains stationary   D. contracts

24. A gallon of water which is changed to steam at atmosphere pressure will increase in vol-   24._____
ume about _____ times.

    A. 5   B. 15   C. 150   D. 1500

25. The humidity of the air means its   25._____

    A. clarity   B. weight
    C. dust content   D. moisture content

26. The safety device which opens automatically to release excessive steam pressure in a   26._____
boiler is the _____ valve.

    A. check   B. safety
    C. gate   D. quick opening

27. Of the following devices, the one which is NOT usually found on a natural draft coal-fired   27._____
boiler is the

    A. feedwater regulator   B. low-water cutout
    C. safety valve   D. water column

28. The number of degree days for two days in the city when the temperature for these two days averages 55° F is   28.____

    A. 2   B. 10   C. 20   D. 30

29. A detergent is GENERALLY used in   29.____

    A. waterproofing walls
    B. killing crabgrass
    C. cleaning floor and walls
    D. exterminating rodents

30. The MAIN reason for using a sweeping compound is to   30.____

    A. spot-finish waxed surfaces
    B. retard dust when sweeping floors
    C. loosen accumulations of grease
    D. remove paint spots from tile flooring

31. The one of the following cleaning agents which is RECOMMENDED for use on marble floors is   31.____

    A. an acid cleaner
    B. a soft soap
    C. trisodium phosphate
    D. a neutral liquid detergent

32. A cleaning solution of one cup of soap chips dissolved in a pail of warm water can be used to wash   32.____

    A. painted walls   B. rubber tile
    C. marble walls   D. terrazzo floors

33. Sodium fluoride is a   33.____

    A. pesticide   B. disinfectant
    C. detergent   D. paint thinner

34. Scratches or burns in linoleum, rubber tile, or cork floors should be removed by rubbing with   34.____

    A. crocus cloth   B. fine steel wool
    C. sandpaper   D. emery cloth

35. A room 12 feet wide by 25 feet long has a floor area of _____ square feet.   35.____

    A. 37   B. 200   C. 300   D. 400

36. A cleaning solution should be applied to a painted wall using a   36.____

    A. wool rag   B. brush   C. sponge   D. squeegee

37. When scrubbing a wooden floor, it is advisable to   37._____

   A. flood the surface with the cleaning solution in order to float the dirt out of all cracks and crevices
   B. hose off the loosened dirt before starting the scrubbing operation
   C. pick up the cleaning solution as soon as possible
   D. mix a mild acid with the cleaning solution in order to clean the surface quickly

38. How many hours will it take a worker to sweep a floor space of 2800 square feet if he sweeps at the rate of 800 square feet per hour?   38._____

   A. 8   B. 6 1/2   C. 3 1/2   D. 2 1/2

39. One gallon of water contains   39._____

   A. 2 quarts   B. 4 quarts   C. 2 pints   D. 4 pints

40. A standard cleaning solution is prepared by mixing 4 ounces of detergent powder in 2 gallons of water.   40._____
The number of ounces of detergent powder needed, for the same strength solution, in 5 gallons of water is

   A. 4   B. 6   C. 8   D. 10

———————

KEY (CORRECT ANSWERS)

1.	A	11.	A	21.	A	31.	D
2.	B	12.	C	22.	B	32.	A
3.	A	13.	C	23.	B	33.	A
4.	B	14.	D	24.	D	34.	B
5.	C	15.	D	25.	D	35.	C
6.	A	16.	B	26.	B	36.	C
7.	A	17.	A	27.	B	37.	C
8.	C	18.	C	28.	C	38.	C
9.	C	19.	C	29.	C	39.	B
10.	D	20.	C	30.	B	40.	D

———————

TEST 2

DIRECTIONS: Each question or incomplete statement is followed by several suggested answers or completions. Select the one that BEST answers the question or completes the statement. *PRINT THE LETTER OF THE CORRECT ANSWER IN THE SPACE AT THE RIGHT.*

1. A custodian should know approximately how long it takes to do each job so that he can   1.____

   A. judge correctly if the person doing the job is working too slowly
   B. tell how much time to take if he has to do it himself
   C. retrain experienced employees in better work habits
   D. tell how much time to dock a worker if he skips that part of the work

2. In order to have building employees willing to follow standardized cleaning procedures, the custodian must be prepared to   2.____

   A. demonstrate the advantages of the procedures
   B. do part of the cleaning work each day until the employees learn the procedures
   C. let the employees go home early if they save time using the procedures
   D. offer incentive pay to encourage their use

3. The BEST agent to use to remove chewing gum from fabric is   3.____

   A. ammonia   B. chlorine bleach
   C. a degreaser   D. water

4. Water emulsion wax should NOT be used on   4.____

   A. linoleum   B. cork tile flooring
   C. furniture   D. rubber tile flooring

5. Tops of desks, file cabinets, and bookcases are BEST dusted with a   5.____

   A. damp cloth   B. treated cotton cloth
   C. damp sponge   D. feather duster

6. The one of the following which is NOT a material used in scrub brushes is   6.____

   A. tampico   B. terrazzo   C. palmetto   D. bassine

7. A chamois is PROPERLY used to   7.____

   A. wash enamel surfaces   B. wash window glass
   C. dry enamel surfaces   D. dry window glass

8. The PROPER sequence of operations used in cleaning an office, when the floor is to be ' swept with a broom, is   8.____

   A. clean ashtrays, empty wastebaskets, sweep, dust
   B. sweep, dust, clean ashtrays, empty wastebaskets
   C. dust, sweep, clean ashtrays, empty wastebaskets
   D. clean ashtrays, empty wastebaskets, dust, sweep

9. Of the following, the MOST common result of accidents occurring while using hand tools is   9._____

    A. loss of limbs   B. loss of eyesight
    C. infection of wounds   D. loss of life

10. A twenty-four foot long extension ladder is placed with its top resting against a vertical wall.   10._____
The SAFEST procedure would be to place the base of the ladder a distance from the wall of _____ feet.

    A. 3   B. 6   C. 9   D. 12

11. The one of the following extinguishing agents which should NOT be used on an oil fire is   11._____

    A. foam   B. sand
    C. water   D. carbon dioxide

12. The extinguishing agent in a portable soda-acid fire extinguisher is   12._____

    A. sodium bicarbonate   B. sulphuric acid
    C. carbon dioxide   D. water

13. The information on an accident report which is MOST useful toward prevention of similar accidents is the   13._____

    A. name of the victim
    B. cause of the accident
    C. type of injury sustained
    D. date of the accident

14. A fusible link is used to   14._____

    A. weld two pieces of chain together
    B. solder an electric wire to a terminal
    C. attach a ground wire to a water pipe
    D. hold a fire door open

15. When making up a pipe joint in the shop, between a nipple and a valve, the _____ should be held in a _____ vise and the _____ .   15._____

    A. valve; square-jawed; pipe screwed into it
    B. pipe; square-jawed; valve screwed onto it
    C. valve; pipe; pipe screwed into it
    D. pipe; pipe; valve screwed onto it

16. A city water meter is USUALLY read in   16._____

    A. pounds   B. cubic feet
    C. pounds per square inch   D. degrees

17. The valve which AUTOMATICALLY prevents back flow in a water pipe is called a _____ valve.   17._____

    A. check   B. globe   C. gate   D. by-pass

18. The BEST wrench to use to tighten a galvanized iron pipe valve or fitting which has hexagonal ends is _____ wrench.   18._____

    A. stillson   B. strap   C. monkey   D. socket

19. A flushometer would be connected to a   19._____

    A. water meter   B. toilet bowl
    C. garden hose   D. fire hose

20. Electric service meters are read in   20._____

    A. kilowatt hours   B. electrons
    C. amperes   D. volts

21. The device used to reduce the voltage of an electric circuit is the   21._____

    A. voltmeter   B. fuse
    C. circuit breaker   D. transformer

22. Ordinary light bulbs are USUALLY rated in   22._____

    A. watts   B. ohms   C. amperes   D. filaments

23. The electric plug on a scrubbing machine should be plugged into a   23._____

    A. light socket   B. wall outlet
    C. fuse receptacle   D. dimmer switch

24. The device which should be used to connect the output shaft of an electric motor to the input shaft of the centrifugal pump is the   24._____

    A. flexible coupling   B. petcock
    C. alemite fitting   D. clutch

25. The type of wood screw which is used to attach a hinge to a door jamb is the _____ screw.   25._____

    A. flat head   B. lag
    C. round head   D. square head

26. Of the following bolt sizes, the one which identifies the bolt that has the LARGEST diameter is   26._____

    A. 4 - 40   B. 6 - 32   C. 8 - 32   D. 10 - 24

27. The tool MOST commonly used with a mitre box to cut wooden molding is the _____ saw.   27._____

    A. hack   B. rip   C. keyhole   D. back

28. The type of lock which can be opened ONLY from the lock side of a door is the   28._____

    A. cylinder lock   B. spring latch
    C. padlock   D. mortise lock

29. A key which will open many locks of the same type is USUALLY called a _____ key.   29._____

    A. tumbler   B. master   C. magnetic   D. cotter

30. Of the following, the BEST lubricant to use on locks is   30.____

    A. grease   B. graphite
    C. mineral oil   D. talc

31. A device which allows an exit door to be opened from the inside by pressing on a horizontal bar is known as a   31.____

    A. door pull   B. double bolt bar lock
    C. cross bolt dead lock   D. panic bolt

32. The MOST useful information for preventing future vandalism which should be included in a vandalism report is   32.____

    A. a list of damaged items
    B. how the vandals got into the building
    C. a list of stolen items
    D. how many hours it took to clean up the mess

33. A custodian should tour his assigned building a short time after the closing time MAINLY to see that   33.____

    A. any office workers who are on overtime are really working
    B. no unauthorized persons are in the building
    C. all the hall lights are turned off
    D. all the typewriters have dust covers on

34. As a custodian, if you want to be sure that a worker understands some difficult job instructions you just gave him, it is MOST important for you to   34.____

    A. ask him questions about the instructions
    B. ask him to write the instructions down and show them to you
    C. ask an experienced man to check on his work
    D. check on his work yourself after he has finished

35. The BEST way for a custodian to keep control of his work assignments is to   35.____

    A. inspect the building weekly
    B. make a written schedule and check it against the work being done each day
    C. have the men report to him at the completion of each job and then give them a new assignment
    D. leave the men on their own until complaints are received

36. The MOST important thing a custodian must do is to   36.____

    A. plan ahead
    B. keep stock records
    C. put out the lights when leaving the building
    D. answer the telephone

37. One of the ways in which a custodian can maintain proper control of his subordinates is to   37.____

    A. punish every minor infraction of the rules
    B. deny making any mistakes himself

C. criticize his own supervisor to show his own superiority
D. instill the idea that he keeps an eye on everything in his department

38. You see that one of your workers is not doing a job according to the safety rules. You should

38.____

A. correct him so that he will know how to work
B. take him off the job and send him to training class
C. let it go and wait to see if he works this way all the time
D. bawl him out

39. The BEST action a custodian can take to promote the security of his building is to

39.____

A. depend on the police department to constantly patrol the area
B. turn out all outside lights so that it will be difficult for intruders to find entry at night
C. be sure all doors and windows are locked securely before the last person leaves the building at night
D. allow only employees to enter the building during the day

40. The one thing a custodian should NOT do after his building has been broken into is to

40.____

A. notify the police
B. report the incident to his supervisor
C. leave the damage to doors or windows unrepaired until his supervisor can inspect them on his regularly scheduled visit
D. make the point of entry more secure than it was before the break-in

––––––––––

KEY (CORRECT ANSWERS)

1.	A	11.	C	21.	D	31.	D
2.	A	12.	D	22.	A	32.	B
3.	C	13.	B	23.	B	33.	B
4.	C	14.	D	24.	A	34.	A
5.	B	15.	D	25.	A	35.	B
6.	B	16.	B	26.	D	36.	A
7.	D	17.	A	27.	D	37.	D
8.	A	18.	C	28.	C	38.	A
9.	C	19.	B	29.	B	39.	C
10.	B	20.	A	30.	B	40.	C

––––––––––

EXAMINATION SECTION
TEST 1

DIRECTIONS: Each question or incomplete statement is followed by several suggested answers or completions. Select the one that BEST answers the question or completes the statement. *PRINT THE LETTER OF THE CORRECT ANSWER IN THE SPACE AT THE RIGHT.*

1. There are a considerable number of forms and reports to be submitted on schedule by a building custodian.
The ADVISABLE method of accomplishing this duty is to

    A. fill out the reports at odd times during the days when you have free time
    B. schedule a definite period of the work week for completing these forms and reports
    C. assign your foreman or cleaner to handle all these forms for you and to have them available on time
    D. classify or group the forms and reports and fill out only one of each group and refer the other forms or reports to the ones completed

1.____

2. In enforcing compliance with safety regulations, you should take the attitude that they must be complied with because

    A. every accident can be prevented
    B. safety regulations are based on reason and experience with the best methods of accident prevention
    C. compliance with safety regulations will make other safety efforts unnecessary
    D. they are the law, and law enforcement is an end in itself

2.____

3. The use of trisodium phosphate in cleaning marble should be avoided because

    A. it discolors the surface of the marble
    B. the salt crystals get in the pores, expand, and crack the marble
    C. it pits the glazed surface and bleaches the marble
    D. it builds up a slick surface on the marble

3.____

4. The use of a concentrated cleaning solution on painted or varnished woodwork

    A. results in burning the pigments of paint or varnish, causing dull, streaky surfaces
    B. cuts down on time and energy in maintaining clean, unblemished surfaces
    C. insures spotless, clean, bright surfaces
    D. is detrimental to the health of the cleaners

4.____

5. A building custodian will make the BEST impression on the office staff if he

    A. impresses them with the importance of his job
    B. says little and is cold and distant
    C. is easy-going and good-natured
    D. is courteous and performs his duties with as little delay as possible

5.____

6. Domestic hot water storage reservoirs should be thoroughly cleaned once

    A. a week   B. a month
    C. a year   D. every two years

6.____

7. A *pH* value of 4 would indicate a(n)   7.___

    A. acid solution   B. neutral solution
    C. alkaline solution   D. low pressure heating system

8. When the diaphragm or bellows of a thermostatic radiator trap is found to be dirty, it is   8.___
    USUALLY cleaned with

    A. turpentine   B. carbon tetrachloride
    C. kerosene   D. mild soap and water

9. The CHIEF purpose of a plumbing trap is to   9.___

    A. permit air to enter the sewer
    B. prevent the entrance of sewer gas into the building
    C. break the shock of the water draining off
    D. siphon off the waste water

10. The safety device on the gas pilot flame of a gas-fired apparatus should operate on pilot   10.___
     flame failure to

    A. bypass the main gas supply directly to the flue
    B. switch over to auxiliary bottled gas pilot flame
    C. shut off the gas supply
    D. introduce sufficient excess air to keep the furnace below the lower explosive limit

11. When instructing employees in regard to their duties in case of fire, a supervisor should   11._

    A. tell employees to take no action until the fire department equipment has arrived
    B. tell all employees to go to the scene of the fire
    C. assign each employee specific duties
    D. tell employees to extinguish the fire before calling the supervisor or the fire depart-
        ment

12. The PRINCIPAL value of a good report is that it   12.___

    A. is always available for reference
    B. impresses department heads with the need for immediate action
    C. reflects upon the writer of the report
    D. expedites official business

13. The quality of work performed by personnel engaged in building cleaning is BEST evalu-   13.___
     ated by

    A. studying building cleaning expenditures
    B. studying time records of personnel
    C. analyzing complaints by building occupants
    D. inspecting the building periodically

14. Of the following, a building custodian need NOT be kept informed on   14.___

    A. departmental management policies
    B. terms of union contracts covering his subordinates
    C. developments of current interest in custodial operations
    D. current rate of interest on municipal bonds

15. The BEST way to make work assignments to persons required to clean a multi-story building is to   15.____

    A. allow the persons to pick their room or area assignments out of a hat
    B. make specific room or area assignments to each person separately
    C. rotate room and area assignments daily according to a chart posted on the bulletin board
    D. each week let a different member of the group make the room or area assignment

16. One important use of accident reports is to provide information that may be used to reduce the possibility of similar accidents.
The MOST valuable entry on the report for this purpose is the   16.____

    A. name of the victim
    B. injury sustained by the victim
    C. cause of the accident
    D. location of the accident

17. Suppose that an emergency has arisen which requires you to cancel some of the jobs scheduled for that day.
Of the following jobs, the one that can be eliminated for that day with LEAST effect on the proper operation and maintenance of the building is   17.____

    A. mopping and cleaning toilet rooms
    B. checking public stairs and corridors for hazards
    C. improving the location of supplies in the storeroom
    D. replacing broken window panes in offices

18. Of the following, a building custodian's attitude toward grievances should be to   18.____

    A. pay little attention to little grievances
    B. be very alert to grievances and make adjustments in existing conditions to appease all of them
    C. know the most frequent causes of grievances and strive to prevent them from arising
    D. maintain rigid discipline of a nature that *smoothes out* all grievances

19. A heavy snowfall must be removed from the sidewalks around the building. You, as building custodian, have assigned two men to shovel snow from the walks. After an interval, you check and find they are bickering as to how much each is shoveling, and no snow is being removed.
In this situation, you should   19.____

    A. stand with them to supervise the snow removal and to be sure the work is divided evenly
    B. assign two other men to snow removal and send the original two back to their usual chores
    C. put the man with seniority in full charge of the other man
    D. separate the men by sending them to opposite ends of the walks to shovel alone, with a warning that you will be checking on their progress at short intervals

20. Of the following, safety on the job is BEST assured by   20._____

     A. keeping alert   B. following every rule
     C. working very slowly   D. never working alone

_____

KEY (CORRECT ANSWERS)

1.	B		11.	C
2.	B		12.	D
3.	B		13.	D
4.	A		14.	D
5.	D		15.	B
6.	C		16.	C
7.	A		17.	C
8.	C		18.	C
9.	B		19.	D
10.	C		20.	A

_____

TEST 2

DIRECTIONS: Each question or incomplete statement is followed by several suggested answers or completions. Select the one that BEST answers the question or completes the statement. *PRINT THE LETTER OF THE CORRECT ANSWER IN THE SPACE AT THE RIGHT.*

1. A foam-type fire extinguisher extinguishes fires by   1.____

   A. cooling *only*   B. drenching *only*
   C. smothering *only*   D. cooling and smothering

2. The extinguishing agent in a soda-acid fire extinguisher is   2.____

   A. carbon dioxide   B. water
   C. carbon tetrachloride   D. calcium chloride solution

3. The PROPER extinguisher to use on an electrical fire in an operating electric motor is 3.____

   A. foam   B. carbon dioxide
   C. soda and acid   D. water

4. When an extension ladder is in place and ready to be used, the rope used to extend the 4.____
   ladder should be

   A. left hanging free out of the way of the climber's feet
   B. used to raise and lower tools to the man on the ladder
   C. used as a means of steadying the climber
   D. tied securely around a lower rung

5. The PRINCIPAL characteristic of panic locks or bolts on doors of places of public assem- 5.____
   bly is that they

   A. allow the doors to open outwardly with sufficient pressure on the bars of the lock
   B. allow the doors to open inwardly with sufficient pressure on the bars of the lock
   C. prevent the door from opening under impact load
   D. may be opened with any tumbler lock key

6. The MAIN purpose of periodic inspections and tests of electrical equipment is to   6.____

   A. encourage the men to take better care of the equipment
   B. make the men familiar with the equipment
   C. discover minor faults before they develop into major faults
   D. keep the men busy during otherwise slack periods

7. Standard, extra strong, and double extra strong welded steel pipe of a given size all have 7.____
   the SAME

   A. outside diameter
   B. inside diameter
   C. average diameter
   D. flow capacity for any given flow velocity

8. In reference to domestic gas piping, 8.___

    A. couplings with running threads are used to join pipes
    B. risers must have a drip leg and cap at bottom
    C. gasketed unions may be used in joining pipe
    D. composition disc globe valves are used to throttle the gas

9. Chewing gum should be removed from rubber, asphalt, or linoleum flooring with 9.___

    A. a putty knife   B. steel wool
    C. gritty compounds   D. a solvent

10. Which one of the following is the BEST procedure to follow when the linoleum floor of a 10.___
meeting room containing movable furniture is to be mopped?

    A. The furniture should be moved by sliding it along the floor to prevent injury to the
       cleaners.
    B. The furniture should not be moved.
    C. The furniture should be moved by lifting it and carrying it to a clear spot to prevent
       damage to the linoleum.
    D. Very little water should be used in order to prevent the legs of the furniture from
       getting wet.

11. Asphalt tile flooring that has been subjected to oily compounds 11.___

    A. may last indefinitely
    B. must be removed and replaced with new asphalt tile immediately
    C. may be restored to hardness and lustre by several moppings with hot water and
       several applications of water wax
    D. must be restored to original condition by several moppings with kerosene

12. The use of alcohol in water for washing windows is NOT recommended because it 12.___

    A. is a hazard to the cleaner in that he may be affected by the fumes
    B. will damage the paint around the edges of the glass
    C. pits the surface of the glass
    D. destroys the bristles of the brush applying the solution to the pane

13. Of the following, the BEST material to use for removing grass stains on marble or wood 13.___
is

    A. oxalic acid   B. chloride of lime
    C. sodium silicate   D. sodium hypochlorite

14. Shades or Venetian blinds are PREFERABLY cleaned with a 14.___

    A. feather duster   B. counter brush
    C. damp sponge   D. vacuum cleaner

15. Asphalt tile floors are PREFERABLY polished with 15.___

    A. water emulsion wax   B. wax in solution with benzol
    C. a high fatty acid soap   D. sodium metaphosphate

16. Washing soda is used to   16.____

    A. eliminate the need for rinse mopping or wiping
    B. make the cleaning compound abrasive
    C. decrease the wetting power of water
    D. increase the wetting power of water

17. Varnish or lacquer may be used as a sealer on floors finished with   17.____

    A. asphalt tiles   B. linoleum
    C. rubber tiles   D. cork tiles

18. A long-handled deck scrub brush is MOST effective when scrubbing   18.____

    A. large open areas   B. stair treads
    C. small flat areas   D. long corridors

19. The BEST method for preventing the infestation of a building by rats is to   19.____

    A. use cats
    B. use rat traps
    C. eliminate rat harborages in the building
    D. use poisoned bait

20. The one of the following foodstuffs which, if allowed to remain on ordinary asphalt tile,   20.____
will MOST likely be most injurious to it is

    A. milk   B. maple syrup
    C. ketchup   D. salad oil

KEY (CORRECT ANSWERS)

1.	D		11.	C
2.	B		12.	B
3.	B		13.	D
4.	D		14.	D
5.	A		15.	A
6.	C		16.	D
7.	A		17.	D
8.	B		18.	C
9.	A		19.	C
10.	C		20.	D

TEST 3

DIRECTIONS: Each question or incomplete statement is followed by several suggested answers or completions. Select the one that BEST answers the question or completes the statement. *PRINT THE LETTER OF THE CORRECT ANSWER IN THE SPACE AT THE RIGHT.*

1. Employees engaged in cleaning operations who are issued rubber gloves to protect their hands against caustic solutions should be warned that   1.____

   A. such solution allowed to spill over the glove top into the space between the glove and the hand may damage the skin of the hand
   B. rubber gloves have a very short life in contact with caustic solutions
   C. harmful gases can penetrate the rubber and harm even dry hands
   D. contact of the hands with glove-type rubber for over an hour is harmful

2. Pyrethrins are used as   2.____

   A. insecticides   B. germicides
   C. waxes   D. detergents

3. Water hammer is   3.____

   A. a special hammer used to remove scale from a radiator
   B. caused by water in steam lines
   C. caused by excessive boiler pressure
   D. caused by low water level in the boiler

4. Which of the following is USUALLY used in the construction of a steam pressure gauge?   4.___

   A. Perfect circle tube   B. Venturi tube
   C. Bourdon tube   D. Elastic linkage

5. Usually when a large room is gradually filled with people, the room temperature   5.____

   A. and humidity both decrease
   B. increases and the humidity decreases
   C. and humidity increase
   D. decreases and humidity increases

6. A foot valve at the intake end of the suction line of a pump serves MAINLY to   6.____

   A. maintain pump prime
   B. filter out large particles in the fluid
   C. increase the maximum suction lift of the pump
   D. increase pump flow rate

7. A pressure gauge attached to a standpipe system shows a pressure of 36 pounds per sq. in.
   The head of water, in feet, above the gauge is MOST NEARLY   7.____

   A. 24   B. 36   C. 60   D. 83

8. Of the following, the term *vapor barrier* would MOST likely be associated with   8._____

    A. electric service installation
    B. insulation materials
    C. fuel oil tank installation
    D. domestic gas piping

9. Pitot tubes are used to   9._____

    A. test feed water for impurities
    B. measure air or gas flow in a duct
    C. prevent overheating of elements of a steam gauge
    D. control the ignition system of an oil burner

10. In warm air heating and in ventilating systems, laboratories and kitchens should NOT be equipped with return ducts in order to   10._____

    A. keep air velocities in other returns as high as possible
    B. reduce fire hazards
    C. reduce the possibility of circulating odors through the system
    D. keep the temperature high in these rooms

11. One square foot of equivalent direct steam radiation (EDR) is equivalent to a heat emission of _____ BTU per _____.   11._____

    A. 150; hour   B. 240; minute
    C. 150; minute   D. 240; hour

12. Of the following, the one which is LEAST likely to cause continuous vibration of an operating motor is   12._____

    A. a faulty starting circuit
    B. excessive belt tension
    C. the misalignment of motor and driven equipment
    D. loose bearings

13. The function of a steam trap is to   13._____

    A. remove sediment and dirt from steam
    B. remove air and non-condensible gases from steam
    C. relieve excessive steam pressure to the atmosphere
    D. remove condensate from a pipe or an apparatus

14. The temperature at which air is just saturated with the moisture present in it is called its   14._____

    A. relative humidity   B. absolute humidity
    C. humid temperature   D. dew point

15. If scale forms on the seat of a float-operated boiler feed water regulator, the MOST likely result is   15._____

    A. internal corrosion of the boiler shell
    B. insufficient supply of water to the boiler
    C. flooding of the boiler
    D. shutting down of the oil burner by the low water cut-out

16. The compound gauge in the oil suction line shows a high vacuum.   16.____
This is USUALLY an indication of

    A. a dirty oil strainer
    B. low oil level in the fuel oil storage tank
    C. a leak in the fuel oil preheater
    D. an obstruction in the fuel oil preheater

17. Of the following, the information which is LEAST important on a boiler room log sheet is   17.____
the

    A. stack temperature readings
    B. CO_2 readings
    C. number of boilers in operation
    D. boiler room humidity

18. Pitting and corrosion of the water side of the boiler heating surfaces is due MAINLY to   18.____
the boiler water containing dissolved

    A. oxygen   B. hydrogen
    C. soda-ash   D. sodium sulphite

19. The combustion efficiency of a boiler can be determined with a CO_2 19.____

    A. flue gas temperature   B. boiler room humidity
    C. outside air temperature   D. under fire draft

20. The try-cocks of steam boilers are used to   20.____

    A. find the height of water in the boiler
    B. test steam pressure in the boiler
    C. empty the boiler of water
    D. act as safety valves

_____

KEY (CORRECT ANSWERS)

1.	A		11.	D
2.	A		12.	A
3.	B		13.	D
4.	C		14.	D
5.	C		15.	C
6.	A		16.	A
7.	D		17.	D
8.	B		18.	A
9.	B		19.	A
10.	C		20.	A

_____

TEST 4

DIRECTIONS: Each question or incomplete statement is followed by several suggested answers or completions. Select the one that BEST answers the question or completes the statement. *PRINT THE LETTER OF THE CORRECT ANSWER IN THE SPACE AT THE RIGHT.*

1. The reason for sweating inside a refrigerator cabinet is   1.____

    A.   high percent running time of compressor unit
    B.   high cabinet air temperature
    C.   defective expansion valve
    D.   a poor door seal

2. Of the following ingredients, the ones to be mixed with water to *point-up* the brickwork of   2.____
   a building are: 1 part cement,

    A.   2 parts sand, 3 parts gravel
    B.   3 parts sand, 4 parts gravel
    C.   3 parts sand
    D.   5 parts sand

3. Acid soils can BEST be neutralized by liberal applications of   3.____

    A.   manure   B.   salt
    C.   lime   D.   powdered-basalt

4. Summer blooming flower bulbs should be stored in a _____ place.   4.____

    A.   warm, dry   B.   warm, moist
    C.   cool, moist   D.   cool, dry

5. A certain 31-day month had an average temperature of 45 Fahrenheit.   5.____
   The number of degree days for this month is

    A. 31   B. 450   C. 620   D. 1395

6. While concrete is *curing*, it is MOST desirable to   6.____

    A.   expose the concrete to sun and air as much as possible
    B.   keep the concrete surface moist
    C.   maintain a temperature of not more than 60°F
    D.   maintain a temperature of at least 80°F

7. To join two lengths of pipe together in a solid straight run, the fitting to use is a   7.____

    A.   coupling   B.   tee
    C.   hickey   D.   shoulder nipple

8. New copper flashing that has been soldered should be   8.____

    A.   muriatic acid   B.   plain water
    C.   benzine   D.   washing soda or lye

9. The intercooler of a two-stage air compressor is connected to the compressor between the   9.

    A. two stages
    B. filter and the first stage
    C. second stage and the receiver
    D. receiver and point of usage of the air

10. Both terms *tank* and *close* apply USUALLY to   10._____

    A. electric generator couplings
    B. freon storage units
    C. pipe nipples
    D. ventilation plenum chambers

11. The commercial fertilizer *5-10-5* refers to   11._____

    A. 5% nitrogen, 10% phosphoric acid, 5% potash
    B. 5% rotted manure, 10% calcium chloride, 5% bone meal
    C. 5% soda, 10% tobacco dust, 5% bone meal
    D. 5% tobacco dust, 10% rotted manure, 5% sulphur

12. The slope or slant of a soil line is 1/4" per foot. If this drainage line is 50' long, the difference in elevation from one end to the other is, in feet, MOST NEARLY   12._____

    A. 0.55   B. 1.04   C. 2.08   D. 12.5

13. Oil is used with sharpening stones when sharpening wood chisels in order to   13._____

    A. reduce the effort needed to move the blade over the stone
    B. maintain the oil temper of the steel used for the chisel
    C. flush off the small metal chips and clear the cutting edges of the abrasive grit
    D. reduce the temperature due to friction

14. A maintenance man checking a refrigerator for a freon leak would use a   14._____

    A. soap and water solution
    B. halide torch
    C. glycerine solution
    D. linseed oil and whiting solution

15. A basement floor area of 5000 square feet is under 9 inches of water.
If this 9 inches of water is to be pumped out of the basement in one hour, the required capacity of the portable pump, in gallons per minute, is MOST NEARLY   15._____

    A. 63   B. 470   C. 1020   D. 2810

16. A MAJOR advantage of keeping a perpetual inventory of supplies is that it   16._____

    A. gives a current record of the supplies available at all times
    B. reduces the work required to distribute supplies
    C. avoids the need for periodic physical inventories
    D. shows who is using excessive supplies

17. Employees generally do NOT object to strict rules and regulations if they   17.____

    A. are enforced without bias or favor
    B. result in more material gain
    C. deal with relatively unimportant phases of the work
    D. affect the supervisors more than their subordinates

18. In order to have building employees willing to follow standardized cleaning and mainte-   18.____
nance procedures, the supervisor MUST be prepared to

    A. work alongside the employees
    B. demonstrate the reasonableness of the procedures
    C. offer incentive pay for their use
    D. be adamant in opposing changes in the standardized procedures

19. Of the following, the MOST important step when accepting incoming shipments of stan-   19.____
dard items normally carried in stock is to check the items for

    A. electrical performance   B. chemical composition
    C. quantity delivered   D. mechanical performance

20. The orderly arrangement of supplies in storage USUALLY   20.____

    A. takes too much time to be worthwhile
    B. is important only in large warehouses
    C. is essential for stock selection and inventory purposes
    D. cannot be accomplished when package sizes vary

————

KEY (CORRECT ANSWERS)

1.	D	11.	A
2.	C	12.	B
3.	C	13.	C
4.	D	14.	B
5.	C	15.	B
6.	B	16.	A
7.	A	17.	A
8.	D	18.	B
9.	A	19.	C
10.	C	20.	C

————

READING COMPREHENSION
UNDERSTANDING AND INTERPRETING WRITTEN MATERIAL

EXAMINATION SECTION
TEST 1

DIRECTIONS: Each question or incomplete statement is followed by several suggested answers or completions. Select the one that BEST answers the question or completes the statement. *PRINT THE LETTER OF THE CORRECT ANSWER IN THE SPACE AT THE RIGHT.*

Questions 1-3.

DIRECTIONS: Questions 1 through 3 are to be answered in accordance with the following passage.

Terrazzo flooring will last a very long time if it is cared for properly. Lacquers, shellac, or varnish preparations should never be used on terrazzo. Soap cleaners are not recommended since they dull the appearance of the floor. Alkaline solutions are harmful, so a neutral cleaner or non-alkaline synthetic detergents will give best results. If the floor is very dirty, it may be necessary to scrub it. The same neutral cleaning solution should be used for scrubbing as for mopping. Scouring powder may be sprinkled at particularly dirty spots. Do not use steel wool for scrubbing. Small pieces of steel filings left on the floor will rust and dis-color the terrazzo. Non-woven nylon or open-mesh fabric abrasive pads are suitable for scrubbing terrazzo floors.

1. According to the passage above, the BEST cleaning agent for terrazzo flooring is a(n)   1.____

    A. soap cleaner   B. varnish preparation
    C. neutral cleaner   D. alkaline solution

2. According to the passage above, terrazzo floors should NOT be scrubbed with   2.____

    A. non-woven nylon abrasive pads
    B. steel wool
    C. open-mesh fabric abrasive pads
    D. scouring powder

3. As used in the passage above, the word *discolor* means MOST NEARLY   3.____

    A. crack   B. scratch   C. dissolve   D. stain

Questions 4-7.

DIRECTIONS: Questions 4 through 7 are to be answered in accordance with the information given in the following passage.

MOPPING FLOORS

When mopping hardened cement floors, either painted or unpainted, a soap and water mixture should be used. This should be made by dissolving half a cup of soft soap in a pail of hot water. It is not desirable, however, under any circumstances, to use a soap and water mixture on cement floors that are not hardened. For mopping this type of floor, it is recommended that the cleaning agent be made up of 2 ounces of laundry soda mixed in a pail of water.

Soaps are not generally used on hard tile floors because slippery films may build up on the floor. It is generally recommended that these floors be mopped using a pail of hot water in which has been mixed 2 ounces of washing powder for each gallon of water. The floors should then be rinsed thoroughly.

After the mopping is finished, proper care should be taken of the mop. This is done by first cleaning the mop in clear warm water. Then, it should be wrung out, after which the strands of the mop should be untangled. Finally, the mop should be hung by its handle to dry.

4. According to the above passage, you should NEVER use a soap and water mixture when mopping _____ floors.　　　　4._____

    A.　hardened cement　　　　　　B.　painted
    C.　unhardened cement　　　　　D.　unpainted

5. According to the above passage, using laundry soda mixed in a pail of water as a cleaning agent is recommended for　　　　5._____

    A.　all floors
    B.　all floors except hard tile floors
    C.　some cement floors
    D.　linoleum floor coverings *only*

6. According to the above passage, the GENERALLY recommended mixture for mopping hard tile floors is _____ of hot water.　　　　6._____

    A.　1/2 cup of soft soap for each gallon
    B.　1/2 cup of soft soap in a pail
    C.　2 ounces of washing powder in a pail
    D.　2 ounces of washing powder for each gallon

7. According to the above passage, the PROPER care of a mop after it is used includes　　　　7._____

    A.　cleaning it in clear cold water and hanging it by its handle to dry
    B.　wringing it out, untangling and drying it
    C.　untangling its strands before wringing it out
    D.　untangling its strands while cleaning it in clear water

Questions 8-15.

DIRECTIONS:　Questions 8 through 15 are to be answered ONLY in accordance with the following paragraph.

Many custodial foremen have discovered through experience that there are economies to be *realized* by using discretion when ordering items which are similar to each other. For example, it may be cheaper to order a *Sponge block, cellulose, WET SIZE: 6 in. x 4 3/4 in. x APPROXIMATELY 34 inches long* at $7.00 than it is to order separate *Sponges, cellulose, wet size: 2 in. x 4 in. x 6 in.* at 60¢. It does not pay to *over-order* on floor wax which may turn sour if not used soon enough. An average size college building cannot afford to have extra 30-inch floor brooms costing $19.75 each stored *on the shelf* for a couple of years or to let moths destroy the hair in such brooms if proper safeguards are not used.

8. According to the above passage, the items mentioned which are *similar* are   8.____

    A. floor brooms   B. sponges
    C. floor waxes   D. moths

9. As used in the above paragraph, the term *over-order* means to   9.____

    A. order again   B. back order
    C. order too little   D. order too much

10. Of the items for which prices are given in the above paragraph, the MOST expensive one is the   10.____

    A. 30-inch floor broom
    B. 6 in. x 4 3/4 in. x 34 in. sponge block
    C. 2 in. x 4 in. x 6 in. sponge
    D. floor wax

11. As used in the above paragraph, the word *realized* means MOST NEARLY   11.____

    A. obtained   B. lost   C. equalized   D. cheapened

12. According to the above paragraph, the one of the following which may be damaged by moths is the   12.____

    A. floor broom   B. sponge
    C. cellulose   D. wool cloth

13. As used in the above paragraph, the term *wet size* means   13.____

    A. the chemical treatment given to sponges
    B. the amount of water the sponge can hold
    C. that the sponges must be kept moist at all times
    D. that the measurements given were taken when the sponges were wet

14. As used in the above paragraph, the word *at* means   14.____

    A. near   B. arrived   C. each   D. new

15. As used in the above paragraph, the word *approximately* means   15.____

    A. exactly   B. about   C. economical   D. tan

Questions 16-17.

DIRECTIONS: Questions 16 and 17 are to be answered in accordance with the following paragraph.

Painting is done to preserve surfaces; and unless the surface is properly prepared, good preservation will not be possible. Apply paint only to clean dry surfaces. After a surface has been scaled, which means that all loose paint and rust are removed by chipping, scraping, and wire brushing, be sure all dust and dirt are completely removed.

16. According to the above paragraph, the MAIN purpose of painting a wall is to _____ the wall.   16._____

    A. clean   B. waterproof
    C. protect   D. remove dust from

17. According to the above paragraph,   17._____

    A. chipping, scraping, and wire brushing are the only methods permitted for cleaning surfaces
    B. painting is effective only when the surface is clean
    C. scaling refers only to the removal of rust
    D. paint may be applied on wet surfaces

Questions 18-21.

DIRECTIONS: Questions 18 through 21 are to be answered SOLELY on the basis of the following paragraph.

All cleaning agents and supplies should be kept in a central storeroom which should be kept locked and only the custodian, store-keeper, and foreman should have keys. Shelving should be provided for the smaller items while barrels containing scouring powder or other bulk material should be set on the floor or on special cradles. Each compartment in the shelves should be marked plainly and only the item indicated stored therein. Each barrel should also be marked plainly. It may also be desirable to keep special items such as electric lamps, flashlight batteries, etc. in a locked cabinet or separate room to which only the custodian and the night building foreman have keys.

18. According to the above paragraph, scouring powder   18._____

    A. should be kept on shelves
    B. comes in one-pound cans
    C. should be kept in a locked cabinet
    D. is a bulk material

19. According to the above paragraph,   19._____

    A. the storekeeper should not be entrusted with the safekeeping of light bulbs
    B. flashlight batteries should be stored in barrels
    C. the central storeroom should be kept locked
    D. only special items should be stored under lock and key

20. According to the above paragraph,   20._____

    A. each shelf compartment should contain at least four different items
    B. barrels must be stored in cradles
    C. all items stored should be in marked compartments
    D. crates of light bulbs should be stored in cradles

21. As used in the above paragraph, the word *cradle* means a 21.____

    A. dolly
    B. support
    C. doll's bed
    D. hand truck

Questions 22-25.

DIRECTIONS: Questions 22 through 25 are to be answered SOLELY on the basis of the following paragraph.

There are on the market many cleaning agents for which amazing claims are made. Chemical analysis shows that the majority of them are well-known chemicals slightly modified and packaged and sold under various trade names. For that reason, the agents which have been selected for your use are those whose cleaning properties are well-known and whose use can be standardized. It is obviously undesirable to offer too wide a selection as that would be confusing to the cleaner, but a sufficient number must be provided so that a satisfactory agent is available for each task.

22. According to the above paragraph, 22.____

    A. there are few cleaning agents on the market
    B. there are no really good cleaning agents on the market
    C. cleaning agents are sold under several different brand names
    D. all cleaning agents are the same

23. According to the above paragraph, 23.____

    A. all cleaning agents should be chemically analyzed before use
    B. the best cleaning agents are those for which no claims are made by the manufacturer
    C. different cleaning agents may be needed for different tasks
    D. all cleaning agents have been standardized by the federal government

24. As used in the above paragraph, the word *amazing* means 24.____

    A. illegal
    B. untrue
    C. astonishing
    D. specific

25. As used in the above paragraph, the word *modified* means 25.____

    A. changed   B. refined   C. labelled   D. diluted

KEY (CORRECT ANSWERS)

1.	C		11.	A
2.	B		12.	A
3.	D		13.	D
4.	C		14.	C
5.	C		15.	B
6.	D		16.	C
7.	B		17.	B
8.	B		18.	D
9.	D		19.	C
10.	A		20.	C

21.	B
22.	C
23.	C
24.	C
25.	A

————

TEST 2

Questions 1-3.

DIRECTIONS: Questions 1 through 3 are to be answered in accordance with the following passage. Each question or incomplete statement is followed by several suggested answers or completions. Select the one that BEST answers the question or completes the statement. *PRINT THE LETTER OF THE CORRECT ANSWER IN THE SPACE AT THE RIGHT.*

The method of cleaning which should generally be used is the space assignment method. Under this method, the buildings to be cleaned are divided into different sections. Within each section, each crew of Custodial Assistants is assigned to do one particular cleaning job. For example, within a section, one crew may be assigned to cleaning offices, another to scrubbing floors, a third to collecting trash, and so on. Other methods which may be used are the post assignment method and the gang cleaning method. Under the post assignment method, a Custodial Assistant is assigned to one area of a building and performs all cleaning jobs in that area. This method is seldom used except where buildings are so small and distant from each other that it is not economical to use the space assignment method. Under the gang cleaning method, a Custodial Foreman takes a number of Custodial Assistants through a section of the building. These Custodial Assistants work as a group and complete the various cleaning jobs as they go. This method is generally used only where the building contains very large open areas.

1. According to the passage above, under the space assignment method, each crew GENERALLY   1.____

    A. works as a group and does a variety of different cleaning jobs
    B. is assigned to one area and performs all cleaning jobs in that area
    C. does one particular cleaning job within a section of a building
    D. follows the Custodial Foreman through a building containing large, open areas

2. According to the passage above, the post assignment method is used MOSTLY where the buildings to be cleaned are _____ in size and situated _____.   2.____

    A. large; close together   B. small; close together
    C. large; far apart   D. small; far apart

3. As used in the passage above, the word *economical* means MOST NEARLY   3.____

    A. thrifty   B. agreed   C. unusual   D. wasteful

Questions 4-25.

DIRECTIONS: Each question consists of a statement. You are to indicate whether the statement is TRUE (T) or FALSE (F). *PRINT THE LETTER OF THE CORRECT ANSWER IN THE SPACE AT THE RIGHT.*

Questions 4-8.

DIRECTIONS: Questions 4 through 8 are to be answered in accordance with the information given in the following paragraph.

The removal of fine, loose dirt or dust from desks, chairs, filing cabinets, tables, and other furniture or office machines is called dusting. A yard of clean soft cloth, folded into a pad about nine inches square, is best for dusting. The cloth should be dry since oil or water on the cloth may streak the surface that is being dusted. When dusting a desk, care must be taken to put back in the same place any papers that were lifted or moved to one side. Thorough dusting of an office is important in order for the office to look neat and for the health of the people who work in that office.

4. The removal of fine, loose dirt or dust from furniture or office machines is called dusting.   4.____

5. A pad of cloth twelve inches square is best for dusting.   5.____

6. A dry cloth will streak the surface that is being dusted.   6.____

7. Papers that have been lifted or moved to one side when dusting a desk should be put back in the same place.   7.____

8. It is not important to dust an office thoroughly.   8.____

Questions 9-18.

DIRECTIONS: Questions 9 through 18 are to be answered in accordance with the information given in the following paragraphs.

WASHING OF WALLS

The washing of walls is important since wall-cleaning costs are an expensive item in the operating cost of building maintenance.

There is a right and a wrong way to wash walls. Streaks may be caused by water running down the dry wall below the place where one is working. This can be prevented by first wetting a section of the wall with water, starting at the bottom and working up before starting the actual washing operation with cleaning solution. Then, if the water runs down the wet wall, there will be almost no streaking. While washing a wall, the temperature should be reasonably low so that the water will not dry on the wall and cause streaks. Once the dirt on the wall is moistened, the wall must be kept wet until the dirt is removed. The washing of walls should be done with good sponges. One sponge should be for cleaning on the dirty wall and one for rinsing.

When working with the cleaning solution, start at the top of the wall and use a circular motion of the sponge and hand. Work across a given section first to the right and then to the left, and so on down to the base.

After the dirt has been removed, take clean, cool water and a clean sponge and go over the wall to be sure that it is perfectly clean and that no traces of the cleaning solution remain on the wall. Even clean water drying unevenly on a wall will cause slight streaks which become noticeable on the walls.

9. The amount of money spent to wash walls is a very small part in the expenses of running a building.   9.__

10. To prevent streaks when washing a wall, an employee should FIRST wet the wall, starting at the top and working down to the base of a wall.

10.____

11. If a wall is wet in the right way, there will be practically no streaks caused by water running down the wet wall.

11.____

12. If the walls are washed when the room is hot, streaks can be caused by water drying too quickly.

12.____

13. Once a dirty wall is made wet with water, it should be dried completely before the dirt is removed.

13.____

14. To wash walls properly, an employee should use at least two good sponges.

14.____

15. When washing with the cleaning solution, start at the bottom of the wall and work to the top, using a circular motion of the hand and sponge.

15.____

16. When washing with the cleaning solution, the CORRECT method is to work across each part of the wall going first to the left and ending on the right.

16.____

17. After the wall has been washed with the cleaning solution, it must be gone over again with clean water to remove any solution which is left on the wall.

17.____

18. When clean water is used to wash a wall, streaks will never appear, even if the wall dries unevenly.

18.____

Questions 19-25.

DIRECTIONS: Questions 19 through 25 are to be answered in accordance with the information given in the following passage.

CLEANING ELECTRIC LIGHT FIXTURES

A room may be dark not because there are not enough light fixtures but because the globes are dirty. As frequently as found necessary, and at least once a year, each globe on a light fixture should be taken down and carefully washed. It should be cleaned by using a solution of warm water to which has been added about two tablespoons full of washing soda for each 10 quarts of water. The globe must be thoroughly dried before it is put back or it is liable to crack from the heat of the lamp. At the time the globe is washed, the metal parts of the fixture should be wiped with a rag dampened in plain warm water. Most metal fixtures have been lacquered, and any cleaning solution would tend to destroy the lacquer. The electric light bulb should be unscrewed from the fixture and wiped with a slighly damp cloth. If it is burned out, it should be replaced at this time.

19. Dirty light globes will reduce the amount of light in a room.

19.____

20. Light globes should be cleaned only when the attendant replaces a burned out light bulb in a fixture.

20.____

21. To clean light globes, a solution of cold water and ordinary household ammonia should be used.

21.____

22. If a light globe is not completely dry when it is put back on a fixture after washing, the heat from the light bulb can break the globe. 22._____

23. The metal parts of a light fixture should be cleaned by using a dry rag to which has been added a few drops of a cleaning solution. 23._____

24. Most metal light fixtures have a coating of lacquer on them. 24._____

25. To clean a light bulb in a fixture, it should be unscrewed and wiped with a damp cloth. 25._____

KEY (CORRECT ANSWERS)

1.	C		11.	T
2.	D		12.	T
3.	A		13.	F
4.	T		14.	T
5.	F		15.	F
6.	F		16.	F
7.	T		17.	T
8.	F		18.	F
9.	F		19.	T
10.	F		20.	F

21.	F
22.	T
23.	F
24.	T
25.	T

ARITHMETICAL REASONING
EXAMINATION SECTION
TEST 1

DIRECTIONS: Each question or incomplete statement is followed by
several suggested answers or completions. Select the
one that BEST answers the question or completes the
statement. *PRINT THE LETTER OF THE CORRECT ANSWER IN
THE SPACE AT THE RIGHT.*

1. A custodial assistant takes an average of forty minutes   1.___
   to mop 1,000 square feet of floor.
   The amount of time this custodial assistant should take
   to mop the floor of a rectangular corridor eight feet
   wide by sixty feet long is, on the average, MOST NEARLY
   _____ minutes.
   A. 10   B. 20   C. 30   D. 40

2. An auditorium eighty feet by 100 feet must be swept in   2.___
   one hour.
   If each custodial assistant takes fifteen minutes to
   sweep 1,000 square feet of auditorium area, the number
   of custodial assistants that must be assigned to complete
   the sweeping in one hour is
   A. 1   B. 2   C. 3   D. 4

3. A detergent manufacturer recommends mixing 8 ounces of   3.___
   detergent in one gallon of water to prepare a cleaning
   solution.
   The amount of the same detergent which should be mixed
   with thirty gallons of water to obtain the same strength
   cleaning solution is _____ ounces.
   A. 24   B. 30   C. 240   D. 380

4. The floor area of a corridor 8 feet wide and 72 feet long   4.___
   is MOST NEARLY _____ square feet.
   A. 80   B. 420   C. 580   D. 870

5. A water tank that is 5 feet in diameter and 30 feet high   5.___
   has a volume of MOST NEARLY _____ cubic feet.
   A. 150   B. 250   C. 600   D. 1,200

6. The circumference of a circle with a radius of 5 inches   6.___
   is MOST NEARLY _____ inches.
   A. 31.3   B. 30.0   C. 20.1   D. 13.4

7. Suppose that you are the custodian-engineer and an employee 7.___
   works for you at the rate of $8.70 per hour with time and
   one-half paid for time worked after 40 hours in one week.
   His gross pay for working 53 hours in one week is MOST
   NEARLY
   A. $461.10   B. $482.10   C. $487.65   D. $517.65

8. Suppose that you are the custodian-engineer and one of
   your employees has gotten gross earnings of $437.10 for
   the week, all of which is subject to deductions at the
   rate of 4.8%.
   The amount which should be deducted from the employee's
   gross earnings for the week is MOST NEARLY
      A. $2.10   B. $14.70   C. $17.70   D. $20.97

8.____

9. The directions on the label of a bottle of detergent
   call for mixing four ounces of detergent with one gallon
   of water to make a cleaning solution for washing floors.
   In order to obtain a larger amount of solution of the
   same strength, one quart of the detergent should be
   mixed with _____ gallons of water.
      A. 2   B. 4   C. 6   D. 8

9.____

10. The area of a lawn which is 58 feet wide by 96 feet long
    is MOST NEARLY _____ square feet.
       A. 5,000   B. 5,500   C. 6,000   D. 6,500

10.____

11. In a building which is heated by an oil-fired boiler,
    2,100 gallons of fuel oil were burned in a period in
    which the degree days reached a total of 1,400.
    If all other conditions remained constant, the number
    of gallons of fuel oil that would be burned in this
    building during a period in which the degree days reached
    a total of 3,600 is
       A. 2,400   B. 2,900   C. 4,800   D. 5,400

11.____

12. The instructions for mixing a powdered cleaner in water
    state, *Mix three ounces of powder in a 14-quart pail
    three-quarters full of water.* A cleaner asks you how
    much powdered cleaner he should use in a mop truck con-
    taining 28 gallons of water to obtain the same strength
    solution.
    The CORRECT answer is _____ ounces of powder.
       A. 6   B. 8   C. 24   D. 32

12.____

13. A custodian-engineer wishes to order sponges in the most
    economical manner.
    Keeping in mind that large sponges can be cut up into
    many smaller sizes, the one of the following that has
    the LEAST cost per cubic inch of sponge is
       A. 2" x 4" x 6" sponges @ $.48
       B. 4" x 8" x 12" sponges @ $2.88
       C. 4" x 6" x 36" sponges @ $9.60
       D. 6" x 8" x 32" sponges @ $19.20

13.____

14. Two cleaners swept four corridors in 24 minutes. Each
    corridor measured 12 feet x 176 feet.
    The space swept per man per minute was MOST NEARLY _____
    square feet.
       A. 50   B. 90   C. 180   D. 350

14.____

15. Kerosene costs 60 cents a quart.
    At that rate, two gallons would cost
    A. $2.40   B. $3.60   C. $4.80   D. $6.00

15.____

16. The instructions on a container of cleaning compound states, *Mix one pound of compound in 5 gallons of water.* Using these instructions, the amount of compound which should be added to 15 quarts of water is MOST likely _____ ounces.
    A. 3   B. 8   C. 12   D. 48

16.____

17. Suppose that you are the custodian-engineer and one of your employees has gross earnings of $582.80 for the week, all of which is subject to Social Security deductions at the rate of 4.8%.
    The amount which should be deducted from the employee's gross earnings for the week is MOST NEARLY
    A. $2.80   B. $19.60   C. $23.60   D. $27.96

17.____

18. Suppose that you are a custodian-engineer and an employee works for you at the rate of $11.60 per hour with time and one-half paid for time worked after 40 hours in one week.
    His gross pay for working 53 hours in one week is MOST NEARLY
    A. $614.80   B. $642.80   C. $650.20   D. $690.20

18.____

19. The volume, in cubic feet, of a cylindrical tank 6 feet in diameter x 35 feet long is MOST NEARLY
    A. 210   B. 990   C. 1,260   D. 3,960

19.____

20. A room 12 feet wide by 25 feet long has a floor area of _____ square feet.
    A. 37   B. 200   C. 300   D. 400

20.____

21. How many hours will it take a worker to sweep a floor space of 2,800 square feet if he sweeps at the rate of 800 square feet per hour?
    A. 8   B. $6\frac{1}{2}$ C. $3\frac{1}{2}$ D. $2\frac{1}{2}$

21.____

22. One gallon of water contains
    A. 2 quarts B. 4 quarts C. 2 pints D. 4 pints

22.____

23. A standard cleaning solution is prepared by mixing 4 ounces of detergent powder in 2 gallons of water.
    The number of ounces of detergent powder needed for the same strength solution in 5 gallons of water is
    A. 4   B. 6   C. 8   D. 10

23.____

24. The ceiling of a room which measures 20 feet x 30 feet is to be given two coats of paint.
    If one gallon of paint will cover 500 square feet, the two coats of paint will require a MINIMUM of _____ gallons.
    A. 1.5   B. 2   C. 2.4   D. 3.2

24.____

25. The floor area of a room which measures 10 feet long by   25.
    10 feet wide is _____ square feet.
       A. 20   B. 40   C. 100   D. 1,000

KEY (CORRECT ANSWERS)

1. B   11. D
2. B   12. D
3. C   13. B
4. C   14. C
5. C   15. C

6. A   16. C
7. D   17. D
8. D   18. D
9. D   19. B
10. B   20. C

21. C
22. B
23. D
24. C
25. C

SOLUTIONS TO PROBLEMS

1. (8')(60') = 480 sq.ft. Let x = required time in minutes. Then, $\frac{40}{1000} = \frac{x}{480}$. Solving, x = 19.2 or nearly 20.

2. (80')(100') = 8000 sq.ft. Each custodian can sweep (1000)(4) = 4000 sq.ft. in 1 hour. Then, 8000 ÷ 4000 = 2.

3. (8)(30) = 240 ounces

4. (8')(72') = 576 sq.ft. or nearly 580 sq.ft.

5. Volume = $(\pi)(2.5')^2(30') \approx$ 589 cu.ft. or nearly 600 cu.ft.

6. Circumference = $(2\pi)(5") \approx$ 31.3 sq.in.

7. ($8.70)(40) + ($13.05)(13) = $517.65

8. ($437.10)(.048) $\approx$ $20.97

9. 1 quart = 32 oz. Then, 32 ÷ 4 = 8 gallons of water

10. (58')(96') = 5568 sq.ft., which is closest to 5500 sq.ft.

11. Let x = number of gallons. Then, $\frac{2100}{1400} = \frac{x}{3600}$. Solving, x = 5400

12. (.75)(14)(.25) = 2.625 gallons of water. Let x = number of ounces of powder needed. Then, $\frac{3}{2.625} = \frac{x}{28}$. Solving, x = 32

13. For selection B, (4")(8")(12") = 384 cu.in., and the cost per cubic inch = $2.88 ÷ 384 = $.0075. This is lower than selections A ($.01), C ($.011), or D ($.015).

14. Two men sweep (4)(12')(176') = 8448 total sq.ft. in 24 min. = 352 sq.ft. per min. Each man sweeps 176 sq.ft. per min $\approx$ 180 sq.ft. per min.

15. Two gallons = 8 quarts. Then, ($.60)(8) = $4.80

16. 15 quarts = 3.75 gallons of water. Let x = required number of ounces of compound. Then, $\frac{16}{5} = \frac{x}{3.75}$. Solving, x = 12

17. ($582.80)(.048) $\approx$ $27.96

18. ($11.60)(40) + ($17.40)(13) = $690.20

19. Volume = $(\pi)(3')^2(35') \approx 990$ cu.ft.

20. $(12')(25') = 300$ sq.ft.

21. $2800 \div 800 = 3\frac{1}{2}$ hours

22. One gallon = 4 quarts

23. Let x = required number of ounces. Then, $\frac{4}{2} = \frac{x}{5}$. Solving, x = 10

24. 2 coats means $(2)(20')(30') = 1200$ sq.ft. Then, $1200 \div 500 = 2.4$ gallons

25. $(10')(10') = 100$ sq.ft.

TEST 2

DIRECTIONS: Each question or incomplete statement is followed by several suggested answers or completions. Select the one that BEST answers the question or completes the statement. *PRINT THE LETTER OF THE CORRECT ANSWER IN THE SPACE AT THE RIGHT.*

1. Assume that a certain elevator starter is at work 8 hours a day, which includes 1 hour for lunch and two 15-minute relief periods. The rest of the workday the starter is performing his duties.
   If the starter works 4 days, the TOTAL amount of time the starter will actually be performing his duties is _____ hours.
   A. 24   B. 26   C. 28   D. 32

   1.___

2. Assume that a certain bank of 18 elevators operating at full capacity could move 3,240 passengers an hour from the main lobby.
   The number of passengers that one of these elevators could move from the lobby every 15 minutes is, on the average,
   A. 12   B. 22   C. 45   D. 180

   2.___

3. In a certain agency, the amount of absence due to injury or illness was an average of 6 hours a month for each employee.
   If this agency had 335 employees, the TOTAL number of hours lost in a year due to injury or sickness was
   A. 4,020   B. 20,100   C. 24,120   D. 28,140

   3.___

4. Assume that in a certain building the elevators must handle 16% of the building population during a peak traffic period.
   If the building population is 2,825, the TOTAL number of people the elevators must handle during a peak traffic period is
   A. 396   B. 424   C. 436   D. 452

   4.___

5. From his coin bank, a boy took 3 half dollars, 8 quarters, 7 dimes, 6 nickels, and 9 pennies to deposit in his school savings account.
   Express in dollars and cents the TOTAL amount of money he deposited.
   A. $2.82   B. $4.59   C. $6.42   D. $7.52

   5.___

6. If a roast that requires 1 hour and 40 minutes of roasting time has been in the oven for 55 minutes, how many more minutes of roasting time are required?
   A. 30   B. 36   C. 45   D. 55

   6.___

7. On the first day of its drive, a school raised $40, which   7.___
   was 33 1/3% of its Red Cross quota.
   How much was the quota?
   A. $120   B. $130   C. $140   D. $150

8. When 0.750 is divided by 0.875, the answer is MOST NEARLY   8.___
   A. 0.250   B. 0.312   C. 0.624   D. 0.857

9. The circumference of a 6-inch diameter circle is MOST   9.___
   NEARLY ____ feet.
   A. 1.57   B. 2.1   C. 2.31   D. 4.24

10. An 18" piece of cable that weighs 3 pounds per foot has a   10.___
    total weight of ____ pounds.
    A. 5.5   B. 4.5   C. 3.0   D. 1.5

11. The sum of 0.135, 0.040, 0.812, and 0.961 is   11.___
    A. 1.424   B. 1.625   C. 1.843   D. 1.948

12. If an elevator carries a load of 1,600 pounds uniformly   12.___
    distributed on a 4 feet by 5 feet floor, the weight per
    square foot is ____ pounds.
    A. 98   B. 80   C. 65   D. 40

13. If one cubic inch of lead weighs one-quarter of a pound,   13.___
    the weight of a bar of lead 1" high by 2" wide by 8" long
    is ____ pounds.
    A. 1.8   B. 2.5   C. 3.1   D. 4

14. Assume that 8 mechanics have been assigned to do a job   14.___
    that must be finished in 5 days. At the end of 3 days,
    the men have completed only half the job.
    In order to complete the job on time in the remaining
    2 days, the MINIMUM number of extra men that should be
    assigned is
    A. 2   B. 3   C. 4   D. 6

15. An elevator supply manufacturer quotes a list price of   15.___
    $625 less 10 and 5 percent for ten contactors.
    The actual cost for these ten contactors is MOST NEARLY
    A. $562   B. $554   C. $534   D. $522

16. To find the largest number of passengers, including the   16.___
    operator, allowed to ride in an elevator, divide the
    rated capacity of the elevator by 150.
    According to this rule, what is the LARGEST number of
    passengers NOT counting the operator that may be carried
    in an elevator with a rated capacity of 3,000 lbs.?
    A. 18   B. 19   C. 20   D. 21

17. Suppose that the work schedule for operators is 5 days a   17.___
    week, 8 hours a day.
    In a period of 4 weeks, with no holidays, how many hours
    will you be required to be on duty?
    A. 160   B. 180   C. 200   D. 225

18. Mr. Jones takes $100 to cover his expenses for a week.   18.___
    He spends $3.00 for carfare coming to work and $3.00 for
    carfare going home. He buys a 50¢ newspaper each day
    and spends $8.00 for lunch and $2.50 for cigarettes
    each day.
    How much money does he have left at the end of a 5-day
    work week?
        A. $15.00   B. $27.50   C. $50.00   D. $85.00

19. Twelve hundred employees work in an office building.   19.___
    Twenty percent of these employees work on the 4th floor
    and 25% work on the 5th floor.
    The TOTAL number of employees who work on the 4th and
    5th floors together is
        A. 240   B. 300   C. 540   D. 660

20. An elevator makes one roundtrip every 5 minutes, on the   20.___
    average.
    How many roundtrips does it make between 8:15 A.M. and
    9:45 A.M.?
        A. 12   B. 18   C. 20   D. 22

21. The floor of an elevator car measures 7 feet by 8 feet   21.___
    6 inches.
    How many square feet of linoleum would be needed to
    cover this floor?
        A. 31   B. 42   C. $59\frac{1}{2}$ D. $62\frac{1}{2}$

Questions 22-25.

DIRECTIONS: Each question consists of a statement. You are to
             indicate whether the statement is TRUE (T) or FALSE (F).

22. In a city building, there are 20 elevators. If on one   22.___
    day five percent of the elevators are out of order, the
    number of elevators out of order is 2.

23. An elevator operator puts in 32 hours of overtime in   23.___
    January, 26 hours in February, 10 hours in March, 10
    hours in April, and 27 hours in May. The average amount
    of overtime this operator worked per month for these five
    months is 21 hours.

24. A large city building normally has 45 elevator operators   24.___
    on its day shift. The vacation rules require that only
    1/5 be allowed away at any time. The number of operators
    that may be on vacation at one time is nine.

25. In a six-story city building, there are 13 offices on the   25.___
    first floor, 19 offices on the second floor, 18 offices
    on the third floor, 17 offices on the fourth floor, 21
    offices on the fifth floor, and 23 offices on the sixth
    floor. The total number of offices in this building is
    109.

___

KEY (CORRECT ANSWERS)

1. B	11. D
2. C	12. B
3. C	13. D
4. D	14. C
5. B	15. C
6. C	16. B
7. A	17. A
8. D	18. A
9. A	19. C
10. B	20. B

21. C
22. F
23. T
24. T
25. F

———

SOLUTIONS TO PROBLEMS

1. 4(8-1-.5) = 26 hours

2. Each elevator can move 3240 ÷ 18 = 180 passengers per hour, which = 45 passengers per 15 minutes.

3. (335)(6)(12) = 24,120 hours per year.

4. (2825)(.16) = 452

5. (3)(.50) + (8)(.25) + (7)(.10) + (6)(.05) + (9)(.01) = $4.59

6. 1 hr. 40 min. − 55 min. = 100 min. − 55 min. = 45 min.

7. $40 ÷ $33\frac{1}{3}\%$ = \$40 ÷ $\frac{1}{3}$ = \$120

8. .750 ÷ .875 ≈ .857

9. Circumference = ($\frac{1}{2}$')(π) ≈ 1.57'

10. 18" ÷ 12" = 1.5. Then, (1.5)(3) = 4.5 lbs.

11. .135 + .040 + .812 + .961 = 1.948

12. (4')(5') = 20 sq.ft. Then, 1600 ÷ 20 = 80 lbs. per sq.ft.

13. (1")(2")(8") = 16 cu.in. Then, (16)($\frac{1}{4}$) = 4 pounds

14. 8 men × 3 cars = 50% of work; 24 man-days = 50% of work; 48 man-days = 100%; 24 man-days ÷ 2 days = 12 men per day = 4 extra men

15. ($625)(.90)(.95) ≈ $534

16. 3000 ÷ 150 = 20 people, including the operator. Thus, only 19 passengers are allowed.

17. (8)(5)(4) = 160 hours

18. $100 − 5($3.00+$3.00+$.50+$8.00+$2.50) = $15.00

19. (1200)(20%+25%) = (1200)(.45) = 540

20. 9:45 AM − 8:15 AM = 90 min. Then, 90 ÷ 5 = 18 roundtrips

21. (7')(8$\frac{1}{2}$') = 59$\frac{1}{2}$ sq.ft.

22. False; (20)(.05) = 1, not 2.

23. True. $(32+26+10+10+27) \div 5 = 21$

24. True. $(45)(\frac{1}{5}) = 9$

25. False. $13 + 19 + 18 + 17 + 21 + 23 = 111$, not 109

———

TEST 3

DIRECTIONS: Each question or incomplete statement is followed by several suggested answers or completions. Select the one that BEST answers the question or completes the statement. *PRINT THE LETTER OF THE CORRECT ANSWER IN THE SPACE AT THE RIGHT.*

1. When 60,987 is added to 27,835, the answer is   1.___
   A. 80,712   B. 80,822   C. 87,712   D. 88,822

2. The sum of 693 + 787 + 946 + 355 + 731 is   2.___
   A. 3,512   B. 3,502   C. 3,412   D. 3,402

3. When 2,586 is subtracted from 3,003, the answer is   3.___
   A. 417   B. 527   C. 1,417   D. 1,527

4. When 1.32 is subtracted from 52.6, the answer is   4.___
   A. 3.94   B. 5.128   C. 39.4   D. 51.28

5. When 56 is multiplied by 438, the answer is   5.___
   A. 840   B. 4,818   C. 24,528   D. 48,180

6. When 8.7 is multiplied by .34, the answer is MOST NEARLY   6.___
   A. 2.9   B. 3.0   C. 29.5   D. 29.6

7. When ½ is divided by 2/3, the answer is   7.___
   A. 1/3   B. 3/4   C. 1 1/3   D. 3

8. When 8,340 is divided by 38, the answer is MOST NEARLY   8.___
   A. 210   B. 218   C. 219   D. 220

9. Assume that a helper earns $5.58 an hour and that he works 250 seven-hour days a year. His gross yearly salary will be   9.___
   A. $9,715   B. $9,765   C. $9,825   D. $9,890

10. On a certain map, a distance of 10 miles is represented by ½ inch.   10.___
    If two towns are 3½ inches apart on this map, express, in miles, the actual distance between the two towns.
    A. 70   B. 80   C. 90   D. 100

11. The area of the triangle shown at the right is _____ square inches.   11.___
    A. 120
    B. 240
    C. 360
    D. 480

24"

90°

10"

12. The sum of 1/3 + 2/5 + 5/6 is
    A. 1 17/30   B. 1 3/5   C. 1 5/8   D. 1 5/6

    12.____

13. The sum of the following dimensions, 3'2¼", 0'8 7/8",
    2'6 3/8", 2'9 3/4", and 1'0", is
    A. 9'2 7/8"   B. 10'3¼"
    C. 10'7 3/7"   D. 11'4¼"

    13.____

14. If the scale of a drawing is 1/8" to the foot, then a
    ½" measurement on the drawing would represent an actual
    length of _____ feet.
    A. 2   B. 4   C. 8   D. 16

    14.____

15. Assume that an area measures 78 feet by 96 feet.
    The number of square feet in this area is
    A. 7,478   B. 7,488   C. 7,498   D. 7,508

    15.____

16. If a can of paint costs $17.50, four dozen cans of this
    paint will cost
    A. $837.50   B. $840.00   C. $842.50   D. $845.00

    16.____

17. The number of square feet in 1 square yard is
    A. 3   B. 6   C. 9   D. 12

    17.____

18. The sum of 4½ inches, 3¼ inches, and 7½ inches is 1 foot
    _____ inches.
    A. 3   B. 3¼   C. 3½   D. 4

    18.____

19. If a room is 10 feet by 18 feet, the number of square
    feet of floor space in it is
    A. 1,800   B. 180   C. 90   D. 28

    19.____

20. A jacket that was marked at $12.50 was sold for $10.
    What was the rate of discount on the marked price?
    A. 10%   B. 15%   C. 18%   D. 20%

    20.____

Questions 21-25.

DIRECTIONS: Each question consists of a statement. You are to
indicate whether the statement is TRUE (T) or FALSE (F).

21. Three-eighths (3/8") of an inch is equivalent to .0375".

    21.____

22. A floor measuring 12 feet by 9 feet contains 36 sq.ft.

    22.____

23. A box measuring 18 inches square and 16 inches deep will
    have a volume of 36 cubic feet.

    23.____

24. If the charge for a long distance telephone call is 50¢
    for the first 5 minutes and 7¢ for each minute after that,
    then for 85¢ a person could speak for 10 minutes.

    24.____

25. If 15 gallons of gasoline cost $14.85 and you use up   25.___
    10 gallons, then the value of the gasoline which is
    still left is $4.95.

_____

KEY (CORRECT ANSWERS)

1.	D		11.	A
2.	A		12.	A
3.	A		13.	B
4.	D		14.	B
5.	C		15.	B
6.	B		16.	B
7.	B		17.	C
8.	C		18.	B
9.	B		19.	B
10.	A		20.	D

21. F
22. F
23. F
24. T
25. T

_____

SOLUTIONS TO PROBLEMS

1. $60,987 + 27,835 = 88,822$

2. $693 + 787 + 946 + 355 + 731 = 3512$

3. $3003 - 2586 = 417$

4. $52.6 - 1.32 = 51.28$

5. $(56)(438) = 24,528$

6. $(8.7)(.34) = 2.958 \approx 3.0$

7. $\dfrac{1}{2} \div \dfrac{2}{3} = \dfrac{1}{2} \cdot \dfrac{3}{2} = \dfrac{3}{4}$

8. $8340 \div 38 \approx 219.47 \approx 219$

9. $(\$5.58)(7)(250) = \$9765$

10. $3\frac{1}{2}" \div \frac{1}{2}" = 7.$ Then, $(7)(10) = 70$ miles

11. Area $= (\frac{1}{2})(10")(24") = 120$ sq.in.

12. $\dfrac{1}{3} + \dfrac{2}{5} + \dfrac{5}{6} = \dfrac{10}{30} + \dfrac{12}{30} + \dfrac{25}{30} = \dfrac{47}{30} = 1\dfrac{17}{30}$

13. $3'2\frac{1}{4}" + 0'8\frac{7}{8}" + 2'6\frac{3}{8}" + 2'9\frac{3}{4}" + 1'0" = 8'25\frac{18}{8}" = 10'3\frac{1}{4}"$

14. $\frac{1}{2}" \div \frac{1}{8}" = 4.$ Then, $(4)(1 \text{ ft.}) = 4$ ft.

15. $(78')(96') = 7488$ sq.ft.

16. $(48)(\$17.50) = \$840.00$

17. 1 sq.yd. $= (3)(3) = 9$ sq.ft.

18. $4\frac{1}{2}" + 3\frac{1}{4}" + 7\frac{1}{2}" = 14\frac{5}{4}" = 1$ foot $3\frac{1}{4}$ inches

19. $(10')(18') = 180$ sq.ft.

20. $\$12.50 - \$10 = \$2.50.$ Then, $\$2.50 \div \$12.50 = .20 = 20\%$

21. False. $\frac{3}{8}" = .375"$, not $.0375"$

22. False. (12')(9') = 108 sq.ft., not 36 sq.ft.

23. False. (18")(18")(16") = 5184 cu.in. = 3 cu.ft., not 36 cu.ft.
    Note: 1 cu.ft. = 1728 cu.in.

24. True. The cost for 10 minutes = .50 + (.07)(10-5) = .85

25. True. $14.85 ÷ 15 = $.99 per gallon. The value of 5 gallons
    = (5)($.99) = $4.95

———

BASIC CLEANING PROCEDURES

TABLE OF CONTENTS

BASIC CLEANING PROCEDURES

I. TRASH REMOVAL

PURPOSE: To remove waste from patient and tenant areas in order to provide the highest standard of sanitation; protection against fire, pests, odor, bacteria, and other health hazards; and for esthetic reasons.

EQUIPMENT:

Utility cart
Trash cart
Bucket
Germicidal detergent
Plastic liners (small and large)
Cloths
Gloves
Container for cigarette butts

SAFETY PRECAUTIONS:

1. Must wear gloves.

2. Never handle trash with bare hands.

3. Always empty cigarette butts into separate container that has water or sand in it.

4. If liners are not used, do not transfer trash from one container to another transfer trash into a liner. (Shown in Illustration.)

5. Trash must be separated into two categories: General and Special.
   General

PROCEDURE

General

1. Assemble necessary equipment, prepare ger-micidal solution, and take to assigned area.

2. Put on gloves.

3. Pick up large trash on floor, place in trash container.

4. Close plastic liner and secure with tie.

5. Remove liner and place in trash bag on utility cart or place into trash cart, or other trash collection vehicle.

PROCEDURE

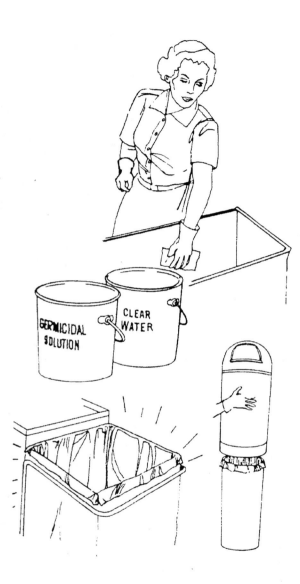

6. Emerge (dip) cloth into germicidal solution. Wring out thoroughly.

7. Wipe outside and inside of trash container. Dry with second cloth.

8. Replace liner. Liner should extend over top of trash container and fold outward over the upper rim. If plastic liners are not being used, use the Replacement Method-a clean container is exchanged for the dirty one.

9. Proceed with this procedure until all trash is collected or containers are full.

10. Place in utility room or an appropriate storage area until time for disposal.

11. Remove trash from the storage area at the end of the day or at some specified time (by cart or dolly) to dumpsters.

12. If large G.I. cans are used in the specified trash storage area, maintain as listed above.

13. At least once a month, take all trash cans to a specified area and thoroughly wash or steam clean.

14. If using the Replacement Method, dirty trash containers must be washed or steam cleaned daily. Must be stored in inverted or upside-down position to air dry.

15. Clean all equipment and return to designated storage area. Restock utility cart.

PROCEDURE

Special
Waste Handling
Syringes-Hypodermic Needles-
Razor Blades

1. Collect from specified areas (full disposable containers designed for this waste).

2. Place in 20-gallon galvanized container
in locked designated area.

3. Call Garage for pick up and disposal
when galvanized container is full (10).

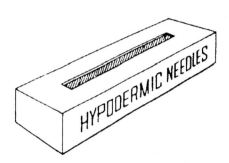

Glass and Aerosol Cans

1. Collect from designated areas in marked
metal containers.

2. Place in 20-gallon galvanized containers
in locked designated area daily.

3. Call Garage for pick up and disposal
when container is full.

Pathological Specimen
(Tissue-flesh)

1. This type of waste is handled by a special technologist in the Hospital's Patho-
logical Division.

2. Must be stored in refrigerator until
incinerated.

3. Must be incinerated in special incinerator
designed for this purpose.

PROCEDURE

Contaminated

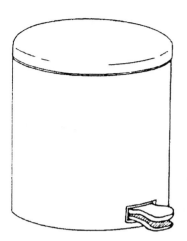

The same procedure is used as for general collection with the following exceptions:

1. Must have covered step-on containers.

2. A second person is required to hold clean liner (top folded over hands for protection).

3. The tied soiled plastic liner is removed from the waste container and placed in a clean plastic liner and then deposited into the regular trash.

4. If in areas that are restricted, must wear protective garments.

II. CLEANING URNS AND ASHTRAYS

PURPOSE: To prevent fire hazards, to control bacteria, and for appearance.

EQUIPMENT:
- Utility cart
- Sifter or slit spoon
- Bucket for sand
- Cloths or Sponges
- Container for cigarette butts
- Gloves
- Buckets (two)
- Counter brush and dustpans
- Germicidal detergent

SAFETY PRECAUTIONS:

1. Wear gloves.
2. Do not place plastic liners on inside of urns.
3. Sweep up all spilled sand immediately.
4. Make sure cigarette butts are placed in special container with water or sand in the bottom.

PROCEDURE

1. Assemble equipment. Prepare solution. Take to designated area.

2. Put on gloves.

3. Empty ashtrays. Dip ashtrays into solution. Wash. Rinse in clear water. Dry. Return to proper area.

4. Continue cleaning other cigarette receptacles. Receptacles can be smoke stands, and/or wall and floor urns with or without sand.

    a. Smoke stands and wall urns:

    (1) Empty cigarette butts into special container (by lifting out inside bucket or unscrewing base from top).

    (2) Wash, rinse, and dry the base, top, bucket and wall attachment.

PROCEDURE

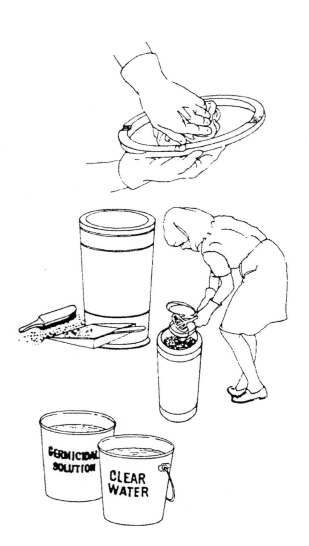

b. Floor urns with sand:

(1) Take out large pieces of trash.

(2) Lift screen to remove cigarette butts and any other waste. Use sifter and spoon for this procedure if screens are not in use.

5. Replace sand if necessary. Sweep up any spilled sand.

6. Dip cloth into germicide solution. Wring out. Wipe off rim and outside of urns. Rinse and dry.

7. Continue this procedure until all urns are completed.

8. Clean all equipment and return to designated storage.

9. At least once a month collect cigarette receptacles. Take to utility room. Remove sand where applicable. Submerge in germicidal solution. Wash thoroughly. Rinse and dry. Replace sand and return to designated areas.

III. DUSTING

PURPOSE: To remove accumulated soil, to control bacteria, for protection, and for appearance.

EQUIPMENT:

    Utility cart
    Treated cloths
    Germicidal detergent
    Gloves
    Furniture polish
    Sweeping tool or Broom
    Extension handle
    Clean cloths
    Buckets (two)
    Vacuum cleaner (Wet and Dry or Back
    Pack) Broom bags

SAFETY PRECAUTIONS:

1. A fold dust cloth is more efficient than a bunched cloth. When folded properly, a cloth may have as many as 32 clean sides.

2. Use treated cloths or damp cloths when dusting. (Never use a feather duster.)

3. Oily cloths are fire hazards: they must be stored in a covered container.

4. Never shake cloth.

5. Never use circular motion. Dust with the grain.

6. Never use excessive water on wood furniture.

7. Do not take dust cloth from one patient unit to the next.

PROCEDURE

General-Dry

1. Assemble equipment. Prepare solution. Take to assigned area.

2. Put on gloves.

3. Fold treated cloth or damp germicidal cloth. (If using the damp germicidal cloth, use a second cloth for polishing.)

PROCEDURE

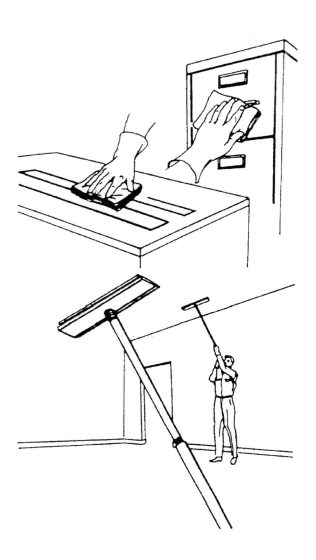

4. Look at area. Begin dusting at a point to avoid backtracking. Use both hands whenever possible. Begin with high furniture and work down to low furniture (for example, dust file cabinets before dusting desk tops).

5. Refold cloth when sides become dust filled or refresh by returning to germicidal solution.

6. Continue dusting until area is completed.

7. Inspect work.

8. Clean equipment and return to designated storage area. Cleaning cloths are placed in liner for laundering; woven treated paper dust cloths are discarded.

Wall and Ceiling Dusting

1. Assemble equipment. Take to assigned area.

2. Move furniture that will interfere with operation to one side of the room. Remove all pictures and other wall mountings and place in a safe area.

3. Put on gloves.

4. Dust ceiling. Start at back of room. Use vacuum or Floor tool or covered broom with extension handle. Place dusting tool against ceiling surface and walk forward to the other end.

5. Turn and overlap stroke. Continue this proc-dure until completed.

6. Dust ceiling both cross-wise and length-wise.

PROCEDURE

7. When ceiling is completed, dust walls from top to bottom. Use full-length vertical overlapping strokes. Include vents, ledges and exposed pipes.

8. When one side of area is completed, replace furniture.

9. Move furniture from other side and continue the dusting procedure until entire area is completed.

10. Replace furniture, pictures and other wall mountings.

11. Inspect work.

12. Clean equipment. Return to designated storage areas. Broom bags are placed in plastic liner/bag for laundering; woven treated paper dust cloths are discarded.

General Comments for Dusting Different Types of Furniture

1. Wooden Furniture:
   a. Dust entire surface.

   b. Apply polish-pour small amount on damp cloth-rub with grain.

   c. Finish polishing by rubbing with dry cloth.

   d. Surface may be washed with natural detergent.

CAUTION: Excessive amount of water should be avoided.

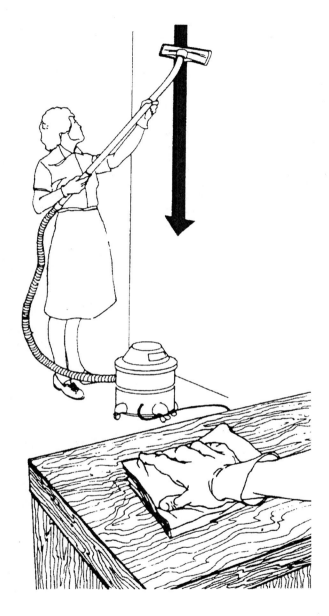

PROCEDURE

2. Metal Furniture:

    a. Dust entire surface.

    b. Surface may be washed and polished.

    c. Apply polish-pour small amount on damp cloth-rub in.

    d. Polish/rub thoroughly with a second cloth.

3. Plastic, Vinyl or Fiber Glass:

    a. Dust entire surface.

    b. Wash with germicidal cleaning solution.

    c. Rinse.

    d. Rub surface dry.

4. Leather:

    a. Damp dust.

    b. Clean with leather polish or saddle soap.

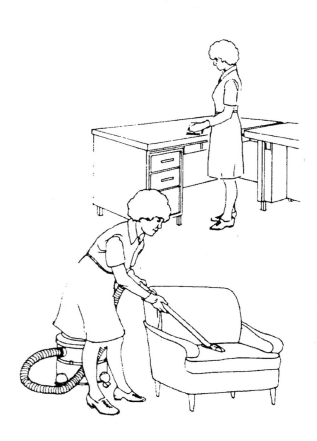

5. Upholstered Pieces:

    a. Vacuum entire surface thoroughly. Use push-pull strokes.

    b. Lift cushion-vacuum both sides, cushion support, and bottom of chair. Do not overlook corners and crevices.

    c. Check carefully for stains and report to supervisor.

PROCEDURE

Naugahyde:

    a. Elastic:

(1) Ordinary Dirt-Ordinary dirt can be removed by washing with warm water and *a* mild soap. Apply soapy water to a large area and allow to soak for a few minutes. This will loosen the dirt. Brisk rubbing with a cloth should then remove most dirt. This procedure may be repeated several times if necessary.

In the case of stubborn or imbedded dirt in the grain of the Naugahyde, a finger-nail brush or other soft bristle brush may be used after the mild soap application has been made.

If the dirt is extremely difficult to remove, wall washing preparations may be used. Abrasive cleaners may also be used. Abrasive cleaners should be used more cautiously and care exercised to prevent contact with the wood or metal parts of furniture or with any soft fabric which may be a part of the furniture.

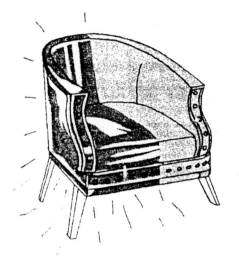

(2) Chewing gum-Chewing gum may be removed by careful scraping and by applying kerosene, gasoline or naphtha. If none of these are available, most hair oils or Three-In-One oil will soften the chewing gum so that it may be removed.

(3) Tars, Asphalts. Creosote-Each of these items will stain Naugahyde if allowed to remain in contact. They should be wiped off as quickly as possible and the area carefully cleaned with a cloth dampened with kerosene, range oil, gasoline or naphtha.

(4) Paint-Paint should be removed immediately if possible. Do not use paint remover or liquid type brush cleaners. An unprinted cloth dampened with kerosene, painters naphtha or turpentine may be used. Care must be exercised to keep these fluids from contact with

PROCEDURE

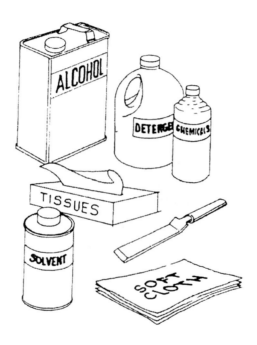

soft fabrics or with the wooden areas of the furniture.

(5) Sulphide Staining-Atmosphere permeated with coal gas or direct contact with hard-boiled eggs, "Cold Wave" solutions and other sulphide compounds can stain Naugahyde. These stains may be removed by placing a clean, unprinted piece of cloth over the spotted area and pouring a liberal amount of 6% hydrogen peroxide onto the cloth and allowing the saturated cloth to remain on the spotted area for at least thirty minutes to one hour. If spot is stubborn, allow the hydrogen peroxide saturated cloth to remain on the spotted area overnight. Caution must be used to see that the hydrogen peroxide solution does not come in contact with stained or lacquered wood and should not be allowed to seep into the seams as it will weaken the cotton thread.

(6) Nail Polish and Nail Polish Remover-These substances will cause permanent harm to Naugahyde on prolonged contact. Fast and careful wiping or blotting immediately after contact will minimize the staining. Spreading of the liquid while removing should be avoided.

(7) Shoe Polish-Most shoe polishes contain dyes which will penetrate the Naugahyde and stain it permanently. They should be wiped off as quickly as possible using kerosene, gasoline, naphtha or lighter fluid. If staining occurs, the same procedure outlined above for sulphide staining using hydrogen peroxide should be tried.

(8) Shoe Heel Marks-Shoe heel marks can be removed by the same procedure as is recommended for paint.

(9) Ball Point Ink-Ball point ink may sometimes be removed if rubbed immediately with a damp cloth using water or

PROCEDURE

rubbing alcohol. If this is not successful, the procedure outlined for sulphide staining may be tried.

(10) Generally stains are found which do not respond to any of the other treatments, it is sometimes helpful to place the furniture in direct sunlight for two or three days. Mustard, ball point ink, certain shoe polishes and dyes will sometimes bleach out in direct sunlight and leave the Naugahyde undamaged.

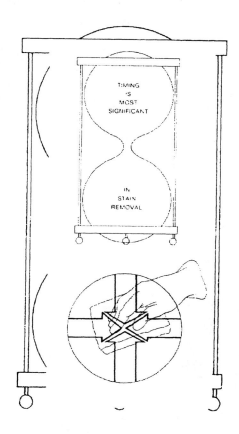

(11) Waxing or Refinishing-Waxing improves the soil resistance and cleanability of Naugahyde. and any solid wax may be used.

b. Breathable:

U.S. Naugaweave should be treated as a soft fabric and not as a fully vinyl coated fabric. U.S. Naugaweave can be cleaned with foam type cleansers generally used for soft fabrics.

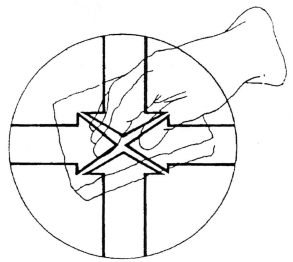

IV. FLOOR DUSTING
(Sweeping/Dusting with covered broom or floor tool with chemically treated disposable floor cloth)

PURPOSE: To remove surface dirt, and make washing easier.

    EQUIPMENT:
- Utility cart
- Dustpan
- Treated cloths, or
- Broom bags
- Counter brush
- Sweeping tool, or
- Vacuum cleaner

SAFETY PRECAUTIONS:
1. Never leave piles of dirt and trash in any area.
2. Lift sweeping tool at the end of each stroke. *Do not tap.*
3. Never put waste or sweepings in a patient's waste basket.
4. Keep all equipment out of traffic areas.
5. Use of disposable cloths should be limited to two surfaces (i.e. use two treated cloths per ward, and two Administrative units can be cleaned with one cloth).

PROCEDURE

1. Assemble equipment. Take to assigned area.

2. Move furniture, if necessary.

3. Start dusting/sweeping at far end of room or area and work toward door.

4. Place floor tool on direct line with right toe. Hold handle loosely. Stand erect with feet about eight inches apart. Start dusting/sweeping floor-walking forward. Use a push stroke, lift tool at end of each stroke. Do not tap. Overlap each stroke.

PROCEDURE

5. Continue this procedure until area is completed. Clean under all stationary equipment and furniture.

6. Take up accumulated dirt. Use dustpan and counter brush. Place in plastic liner/trash bag on utility cart.

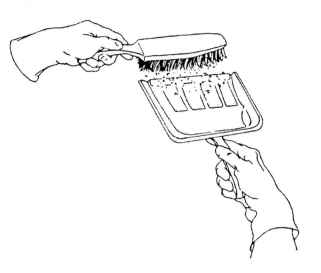

7. The dusting/sweeping procedure can be performed with the wet and dry vacuum cleaner. *Dusting Isolation units must be performed with vacuum.*

8. Inspect work. Floor should not have any dust streaks. Replace furniture.

9. Clean equipment. Return to designated storage area. Discard disposable treated cloths. If broom bags are used, place in plastic liner/bag for laundering.

V. VACUUMING
(Wet and Dry)

PURPOSE: To remove dust and dirt and water, to control the spread of bacteria, to aid in reaching difficult-to-reach areas, and for appearance. This operation may be performed on floors, walls, ceiling, rugs, and carpets.

EQUIPMENT:
Upright or tank vacuum cleaner

Wet and dry vacuum cleaner

Back-pack vacuum cleaner

Attachments: Crevice tool, Shelf brush, Pipe brush, Upholstery brush, Walls and Ceiling brush, Dusting brush, and Floor-dry and wet tools.

SAFETY PRECAUTIONS:

1. Empty vacuum when bag is half full.

2. If disposable bag is not in use, empty soil into plastic liner/bag.

3. Never position equipment so that it becomes a tripping hazard.

PROCEDURE

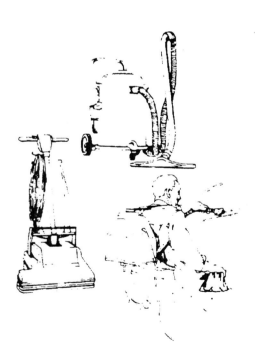

Dry

1. Assemble proper equipment and attachments for the area to be vacuumed:

    a. Upright vacuum for carpet.

    b. Tank cleaner to use on floors, grooves and high cleaning.

    c. Back-pack for stairs, hard to reach areas, walls and ceiling, and drapery.

2. Remove all furniture and other items interfering with the operation.

3. Start in farthest corner of room, area or top of item. Vacuum the surface in a back-and-forth motion.

PROCEDURE

4. Empty bag when half full. Continue this procedure until area or item is completed. Change attachments as required.

5. Replace furniture or items.

6. Take equipment to utility room. Empty and clean. Return to designated storage area.

Wet

This procedure is used to remove water. It is considered very effective in the daily performance of different tasks in order to control the spread of infectious organisms. Wet vacuuming is often used in emergencies-flooding, pipe breaks and overflows. See vacuum cleaner guide under Care of Equipment for operation of the wet vacuum.

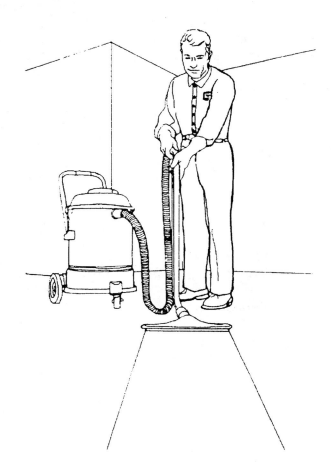

VI . Mopping
(Wet, Damp, Spot)

PURPOSE: To insure maximum cleanliness, to improve the sanitation of the environment, to aid in control of bacteria, and for the appearance of the area.

MATERIALS:

Utility cart
Buckets (two)
Dolly
Wringers (two)
Mopheads and Handles (two)
Nylon abrasive pad
Caution signs
Gloves
Broom-Broom bags
Sweeping tool-treated cloths
Wet and dry vacuum cleaner
Putty knife
Dustpan
Counter brush
Germicidal detergent

SAFETY PRECAUTIONS:

1. Sweep or vacuum before mopping.

2. Post area with "Wet Floor" signs.

3. Mop one-half of corridor at a time.

4. Keep equipment close to walls and away from doors and corners.

5. Excessive water should not be allowed to remain on the floor for any length of time because it will cause damage to nearly all types of flooring material.

6. Begin the operation with clean equipment, mopheads, and clean solution.

7. Change cleaning solution and rinse water frequently (every three to four rooms, depending on size and soilage factors).

8. Solution containers should be conveniently positioned so as not to cause tripping or walking over cleaned areas.

PROCEDURE

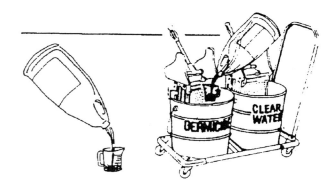

Wet Mopping
1. Assemble equipment. Fill one container two-thirds full with water. Add recommended amount of germicidal detergent. Fill second container two-thirds full with clear water.

PROCEDURE

2. Proceed to designated work area. Post "Wet Floor" signs. Move furniture to simplify operation. Vacuum or dust area with covered broom or tool with treated cloth. Remove gum with putty knife. (Use dustpan and counter brush to remove debris and trash.)

3. Dip one mop into cleaning solution and press out excess water to prevent dripping.

4. First, apply solution on and along baseboard or coving. Use the heel of moptiead to clean baseboard and corners. (The putty knife can be used to clean out heavily soiled corners or strands of the mophead wrapped around gloved fingertips is another tool for cleaning the corners. A baseboard scrubber or an improvised abrasive pad on a mop handle can be used to remove built-up soil on baseboards.)

5. Return mop to germicidal solution. Churn thoroughly, wring out and pick up solution off baseboards. Apply rinse water with second mop and dry.

6. Continue with the mopping operation. Take solution mop (with excess water pressed out) and make an eight-inch border around floor area approximately nine feet wide and twelve feet long.

7. Begin at top of area. Place mop flat on floor, feet well apart, place right hand-palm up, almost two inches from end of handle, and left hand-palm down, about fourteen inches on handle. Begin swinging mop from left to right or right to left using a continuous open figure-eight motion. At the end of approximately six to nine strokes (width of strokes depend on height and weight of worker), turn mop over or renew direction by lapping mop (lift mophead and loop it over the strands). Continue this procedure until area is completed. (A nylon pad attached to one side of mophead can be used to remove black marks while performing the daily mopping procedure.

PROCEDURE

8. Return mop to germicidal solution. Churn thoroughly. Wring out and pick up solution. Use same procedure as for applying solution.

9. Dip the second mop into the rinse water, press out excess water and apply rinse water to area. Use same procedure for rinsing as for applying cleaning solution.

10. Dip the second mop again into rinse water, wring out thoroughly and dry floor using side-to-side stroke.

11. Continue the four steps of mopping, picking up, rinsing, and drying until the area has been covered. Change cleaning solution and rinse water frequently.

12. Inspect work: A properly mopped floor should have a clean surface. There should be no water spots. The corners should be clean and baseboards should not be splashed.

13. Wash and dry equipment and return to designated storage area.

14. Mopheads are removed and placed in a plastic bag, and then placed in a regular laundry bag and stored in the designated area to be picked up and laundered.

PROCEDURE

Damp Mopping

Damp mopping is a type of mopping used to remove surface dust. This procedure may be used in place of dry dust mopping. Each time mop is dipped into solution or rinse water, it is wrung out thoroughly. The same motions are carried out in this procedure as are for the wet mopping.

Spot Mopping

Spot mopping is a type of mopping used only when a small area is soiled by spillage (water, coke, coffee, urine and other liquids). Spillage must be wiped up immediately in order to prevent slipping and falling hazards. First, absorb liquid with paper towels or blotters, then mop area.

WRING DRY

SPECIAL CLEANING PROCEDURES

TABLE OF CONTENTS

SPECIAL CLEANING PROCEDURES

I. DRINKING FOUNTAIN

PURPOSE: To control the spread of bacteria and for appearance.

EQUIPMENT:
  Germicidal detergent

Paper towels
Buckets (two)
Abrasive cleanser
Bottle brush
Cloths
Gloves

PROCEDURE

1. Assemble equipment. Prepare solution. Take to designated area. Put on gloves.

2. Check water flow.

3. Pour some germicidal solution into bubbler/ mouthpiece and inside surfaces.

4. Scrub bubbler inside and outside with bottle brush.

5. Wash inside surface with paper towel. (Use small amount of abrasive cleanser, if applicable.)

6. Rinse with water from bubbler/mouthpiece. Dry with paper towel.

7. Wash outside surfaces including foot pedal.

8. Rinse and dry.

9. Discard soiled paper towels.

10. Continue with next assignment or clean equipment and return to designated storage area.

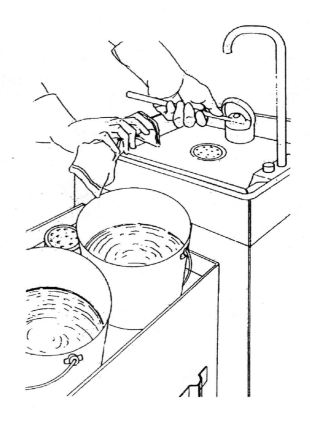

II. MOVING FURNITURE AND EQUIPMENT

PURPOSE: To relocate.

However, for proper maintenance purposes, the Housekeeping Section is involved daily with some form of the moving operation which involves moving of furniture and equipment (desks, file cabinets, beds and other items).

EQUIPMENT: Lifting Aids:
  Desk lifter
  File cabinet lifter
  Dolly
  Cart or Table on wheels
  Blanket
  Straps

SAFETY PRECAUTIONS:

1. Secure all locks and safety adjustments on equipment before using.

2. Remove handles or straps that interfere with the operation.

3. Block or lock all wheels on movable carts or tables.

4. To transport objects on movable table or cart, walk down center of hall; stop at corners, watch swinging doors.

5. Do not block vision.

6. Only properly trained individuals should use specialized moving equip- ment.

General

PROCEDURE

1. Assemble necessary equipment and take to assigned area.

2. Prepare the area (move anything inter- fering with the move).

3. Place lifting aid as close as possible to the piece of furniture or object being relocated.

4. Place object on lifting aid and transport to new location.

5. Return lifting aids and accessories to designated storage area.

PROCEDURE

1. Place under desk and center evenly on arms.

2. Lock. Press down on handle to lift and lock.

3. Remove handle.

4. Move desk to new location.

5. Remove desk lifter. (Insert handle, press down to release safety lock, lower desk into position, and withdraw desk lifter.) Return to designated storage area.

File Cabinet Lifter

1. Adjust bar and lifter head to height of cabinet.

2. Insert lifting blade under file cabinet.

3. Rest lifter head qn top of cabinet.

4. Press lifter tightly against cabinet and adjust arm on the lifter head to fit cabinet top by turning the two wheels.

5. Pull down level on adjustment bar to secure arm and the lifter head.

6. Pivot forward until locked into resting position.

7. Place one hand on bar and the other on handle; press down until cabinet clears the floor.

PROCEDURE

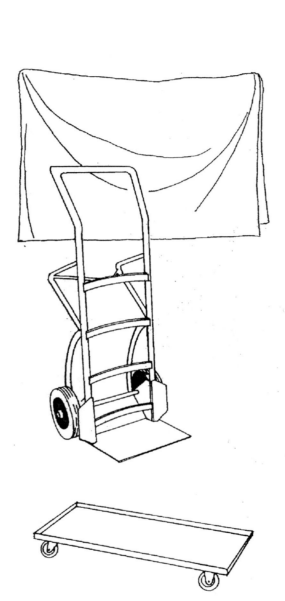

8. Roll into new position.

9. Remove lifter (raise lever arm in upright position, release lifter head by raising the side of the head assembly and remove lifter). Return to designated storage area.

10. To relocate taller cabinets, completely remove the lifter head bar asembly.

- - - - - - - - - - - - - - - - - - -

Other Methods
Blankets, Dollies, Carts or
Tables on wheels

Quite frequently, you may lack the above-mentioned sophisticated equipment. Therefore, you should also know that just by placing a blanket under a desk, table, bookend, file cabinet and other heavy objects, that the item may be pushed or pulled into a new location. If moving over carpeted areas, first place a piece of cardboard down. If using dollies or tables or carts, make sure that furniture or dollies are covered in order to protect from damage.

III. CLEANING DRAPERY, VENETIAN BLINDS AND WINDOW SHADES

PURPOSE: To control bacteria and for appearance.

EQUIPMENT:

    Vacuum cleaner/attachments
    Cart
    Germicidal detergent
    Gloves
    Six-foot step ladder
    Cloths
    Buckets (two)
    Venetian blind brush

SAFETY PRECAUTIONS:

1. Vacuuming should not be done too often, because it weakens the fiber of the fabric.

2. Always cover hands when cleaning Venetian blinds, because of the sharp edges.

PROCEDURE

Drapery

1. Assemble equipment. Take to designated area. Set up ladder and lock.

2. Connect vacuum to nearest convenient outlet.

3. Remove tie-backs and close the draperies.

4. Vacuum. Start at top of cornice or at top of drapery and work down. Use up-and-down motions—overlap.

5. Pull pleats apart to reach all surfaces.

6. Continue this procedure until front of drapery is completed.

7. Pull out drapery and dust the back side. Pull pleats apart to reach all surfaces.

PROCEDURE

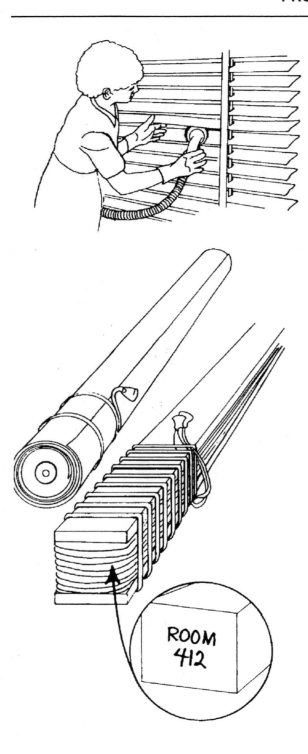

8. Continue this procedure until both panels are completed.

9. Adjust the drapery. Replace ties.

10. Drapery (depending on the type of fabric) is sent out perdiodically to the laundry or dry cleaners. Remove drapes, mark, fold and place in bag. Take to supervisor for cleaning purposes.

11. Clean equipment and return to designated storage area.

- - - - - - - - - - - - - - - - - - -

Venetian Blinds
(Dusting)

1. Assemble equipment. Take to assigned area. Set up ladder and lock.

2. Lower Venetian blind and place in closed position.

3. Plug in vacuum cleaner. Dust tapes.

4. Start dusting heading (stand on ladder if necessary.) Use side-to-side or left-to-right motion.

5. Dust each slat. Make sure to get behind tapes.

6. Continue this procedure until blind is completed. Dust the other side.

7. Adjust blinds and inspect work.

8. Blind may also be damp dusted by hand.

PROCEDURE

9. Clean equipment and return to designated storage area.

Washing

Blinds may be washed at the window or removed and washed in tub, tank, supersonic machine and/or specialized blind washing equipment. Remember to mark blinds if removed for cleaning.

Washing Blinds by Hand:
1. Assemble equipment. Prepare solution. Take to designated area. Set up ladder and lock. Put on gloves.

2. Lower Venetian blind—vacuum.

3. Place slats horizontal.

4. Wash, rinse and dry tapes.

5. Wash heading. Rinse and dry.

6. Dip cloth in germicidal solution. Wring out. Fold around hand.

7. Take slat in covered hand and use a side-to-side motion—moving left to right, cleaning both sides of the blind at the same time (hold slat with one hand while working with the other hand). Avoid too much water.

8. Rinse and dry.

9. Adjust blinds. Wipe up any spills.

10. Remove equipment. Clean and return to designated storage area.

Wash Away From Window:

1. Assemble equipment. Take to area. Set up ladder and lock. Put on gloves.

2. Remove blinds. Pull blinds to top of frame. Unlock the blind from the frame. Wrap or secure the cord around each end. Mark in an inconspicuous place with indelible marker.

3. Place in cart or on dolly and take to area for washing. The blinds may be hung on special racks for washing and rinse with high pressure unit, or may be scheduled to be washed in the blind louvre washing machine that spray washes and rinses blinds in one operation. Blinds are removed from the machine, hung on racks and allowed to air dry.

4. Pull blinds to top of frames. Wrap or secure cord around each end. Place in cart or on dolly and take back to proper location.

5. Install and adjust blinds.

6. Move equipment. Clean and return to designated storage area.

- - - - - - - - - - - - - - - - - -

Window Shades

Window shades require periodic dusting, vacuuming and washing. Most shades are washable. Daily dusting can be accomplished while shade is hanging. It may be performed with a damp germicidal cloth or vacuum cleaner or covered broom.

1. Assemble equipment. Take to designated area. Put on gloves.

PROCEDURE

2. Extend shade full length.

3. Vacuum roller—use side to side motion.

4. Vacuum surface of shade. Use up and down motion. Overlap each stroke.

5. Continue this procedure until shade is completed. If very soiled, repeat procedure using side to side motion.

6. Continue to vacuum opposite side—starting at bottom of shade—hold shade with one hand.

7. Vacuum pull edge—use side to side motion.

8. Vacuum surface—use up and down motion.

9. Roll shade clean on cleaned with one hand and continue the dusting procedure until shade is completed.

10. Adjust shade. Inspect work.

11. Clean equipment and return to designated storage area.

12. Report to supervisor any shade needing repair or replacement.

IV. GLASS AND WINDOW CLEANING

PURPOSE: To remove soil, control bacteria, allow passage of natural light and for appearance.

EQUIPMENT:

Utility cart
Ladder (step or platform)
Buckets (two)
Cloths or Sponges or Squeegees
Gloves
Cleaning agents (Trisodium, Vinegar, Clear water, Alcohol, Commercial glass
cleaners, or Synthetic detergents)
Vacuum cleaner
Cloths (lint-free)
Paper Towels

SAFETY PRECAUTIONS:

1. Make sure ladders are in locked position.

2. When using a six-foot or taller step ladder, a second person is required.

3. Place cloth under the bucket to collect spillage.

4. Do not lean out of windows, sit nor stand on window sills or guard rails.

5. Do not place too much water on wooden frames and sashs.

6. Do not wash windows when sun rays are directly on pane.

PROCEDURE

General

1. Assemble equipment, prepare cleaning solution and take to assigned area. Set up as close to work site as possible. (Make sure ladder is on flat surface and is locked and that a cloth is under the bucket to catch spillage.)

2. Prepare window—Remove objects from sill; remove drapery, curtains, shades or blinds, If there are screens or guards, unlock and vacuum.

3. Put on gloves.

4. Vacuum frame and window sills.

5. Wash window frames—starting at top using

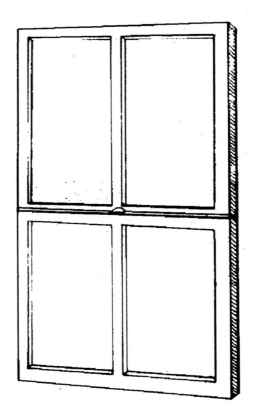

PROCEDURE

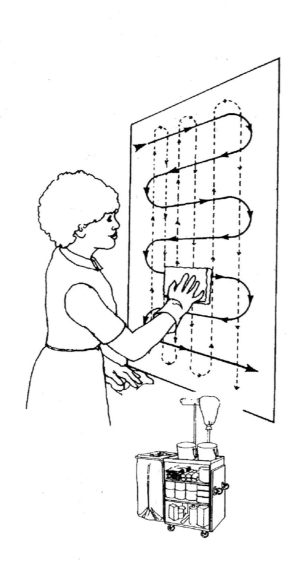

left to right or side to side motion. Then wash the sides using up and down motion.

6. Rinse and dry using same motions.

7. Wash, rinse and dry window sills.

8. Change wash solution, rinse water and cloths. (Clean solution is a necessity.)

9. Dip cloth or sponge into cleaning solution; squeeze out excess water. Start washing at top of window pane (standing to side) using left to right or side to side motion and continue back and forth in one continuous motion until the window is completed. Do not overlook corners. If window panes are very soiled, repeat the washing procedure using up and down motion.

10. Rinse; use the same procedure as washing.

11. Dry with lint-free cloth or paper towel. Use same procedure as for washing. If panes or glass are large or medium in size, use squeegee for drying (using either the "side to side" or "top to bottom" motion) wiping squeegee with cloth after each stroke or when squeegee-pane contact is broken.

12. Continue this procedure until all windows are completed. Then clean equipment and return to designated storage area.

Squeegee Method

1. Apply cleaning solution with sponge or cloth. Use continuous side to side motion.

PROCEDURE

2. Remove water with squeegee. There are two basic motions—*"Side to Side"* and *"Top to Bottom."* Either is acceptable. In the *"Side to Side"* Method, make one continuous stroke starting at bottom of pane with squeegee in flat position and make border. Wipe blade; continue by starting at top of pane (left or right) with squeegee in vertical position; stroke across, and when reaching the opposite side, make a simple half turn overlapping previous stroke. Wipe blade any time squeegee-pane contact is broken. In the *"Top to Bottom"* Method, start at top (left or right corner) of pane and move squeegee to bottom of pane in separate strokes overlapping each stroke. Wipe squeegee blade at the end of each stroke.

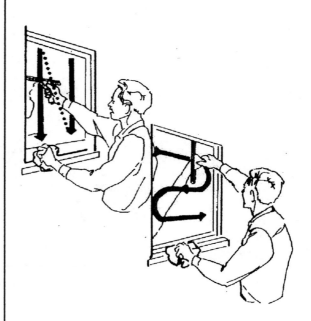

3. Wipe up any spills on the sills or frames.

4. Inspect work. Replace items moved from windows and sills.

5. Clean equipment and return to designated storage area.

Other Glass Cleaning

Entrance door glass is cleaned daily. Use either the general or the squeegee method. Transoms, partitions and desk tops are cleaned periodically. Use procedure as described in the general method.

V. CLEANING OF LIGHT FIXTURES
(Fluorescent and Globes)

PURPOSE: To control bacteria, assure proper lighting and for appearance.

EQUIPMENT:

Utility cart
Cart on wheels
Ladder (safety or platform)
Buckets (two)
Cloths
Germicidal detergent
Treated cloths
Broom block (with extension handle)
Gloves
Broom bags
Vacuum cleaner/attachments
Screw driver

SAFETY PRECAUTIONS:

1. Always turn off light switch.

2. Schedule when there is least traffic.

3. Do not touch light bulbs while hot or with wet hands.

4. Make sure ladder is locked in position.

5. Do not place fixtures where they can be broken.

6. Move any object interfering with procedure.

PROCEDURE

DRY Fluorescent Light Fixtures

1. Assemble equipment, take to work area. Make sure all lights are off.

2. Move furniture if necessary. Choose either the vacuum cleaner or the covered broom with extension handle.

3. Start at the back of the room. Place cleaning tool against side panel and move forward, using side-to-side motion until you reach the end of the fixture. Then do the other side in the same manner.

4. Continue the process until project is completed.

PROCEDURE

5. Clean equipment and return to storage area. Restock utility cart.

- -

Globes
Incandescent Light Fixtures

1. Take assembled equipment and ladder to work area. Make sure all lights are off.

2. Set up ladder and make sure it is locked. If safety ladder is being used, a second person is required.

3. Put on gloves.

4. Dust light fixtures with treated cloth or damp germicide cloth.

5. Clean equipment and return to storage area. Restock utility cart.

- -

WET
Fluorescent and Globes

1. Assemble equipment in designated work area or utility room and prepare solution for washing.

2. Take ladder and cart to scheduled area.

3. Turn off lights.

4. Remove side panels (lift up and out).

5. Remove louvre (egg crates) loosening one side at a time.

6. Take to designated area.

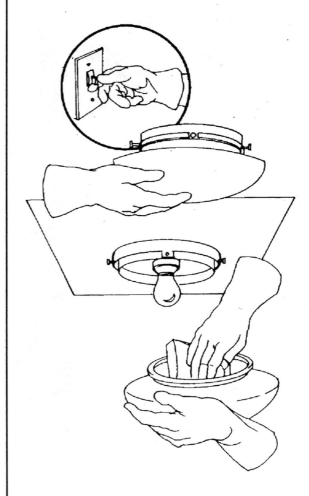

PROCEDURE

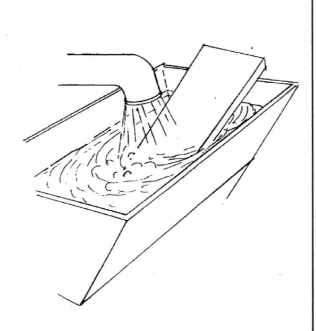

7. Put on gloves.

8. Immerse side panels in prepared solution, wash with soft materials. Don't use any abrasive materials.

9. Rinse in clear water.

10. Dry.

11. Repeat same procedure for "egg crates" and removable incandescent light fixtures (globes). If globes or light fixtures are nonremovable, procedure is to wash, rinse and dry while still attached to the frame.

12. Return light fixtures to their proper area.

13. Attach to frame and make sure that all are securely fastened.

14. Wash and dry all equipment, and return to storage area.

VI. WALL WASHING
(Manual and Machine)

PURPOSE: To remove unsightly soil, control bacteria and for appearance. Walls are also washed for painting purposes.

EQUIPMENT:

Utility cart
Platform ladder or
Step ladder
Cleaning cloths
Gloves
Nylon pad (square)
Drop cloths
Trisodium Phosphate or
Germicidal detergent

Scaffold
Sponges
Buckets (two)
Vacuum (wet and dry or back-pack), and attachments

SAFETY PRECAUTIONS:

1. Areas must be scheduled and the procedure performed when traffic is the least.
2. Secure locking devices on ladder.

PROCEDURE

Manual

1. Assemble equipment. Prepare solution. Take to assigned area.

2. Move furniture to one side of the room or cover it. Remove pictures and other wall mountings. Place in a safe area.

3. Spread drop cloths under portion of wall to be washed.

4. Set up ladder or scaffold. Secure lock if applicable. Put on gloves.

5. If area has not been dusted, vacuum ceiling and walls.

6. Place buckets on cloth on platform (ladder or scaffold).

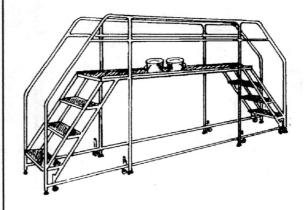

PROCEDURE

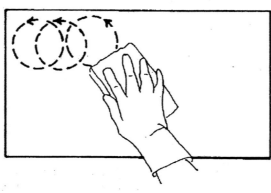

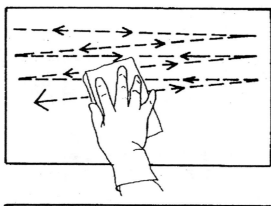

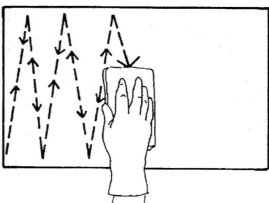

7. Dip sponge into cleaning solution, squeeze out excess water. Take clean cloth to catch drippings.

8. Start at top or bottom. Wash small area. Use circular motion.

9. Dip second sponge into rinse water. Squeeze out excess water. Rinse, use side to side motion.

10. Dry with soft lint-free cloth. Use up and down motion.

11. Continue washing, rinsing and drying until area is completed. Overlap strokes to prevent streaking.

12. Replace furniture. Continue to other side.

13. Move furniture. Continue with the procedure until all walls are washed.

14. Replace all furniture, pictures and mountings.

15. Inspect work.

16. Clean equipment and return to designated storage area.

Machine

The wall washing procedure can be accomplished by machine, thereby saving the institution a great deal of time and labor. The additional equipment necessary to perform this operation includes:

PROCEDURE

Wall washing pressure tanks
Trowels
Wall washing towels
Neutral detergent

SAFETY PRECAUTIONS:

1. Make sure pressure is released before cleaning tanks.

2. Avoid the use of excessive pressure. Excessive pressure will force soil into surface.

1. Assemble equipment. Prepare solution. Take to designated area.

2. Build up pressure in tanks.

3. Place toweling material on trowels.

4. Follow room preparation procedure as in manual wall washing.

5. Dust wall with vacuum.

6. Press solution release levers and thoroughly wet trowels.

7. Begin washing wall. Start by placing trowel in upper corner of wall. Move trowel in a rhythmic side to side motion. Overlap each stroke. Work down the wall by stepping back.

8. Rinse. Use rinse trowel.

9. Dry with third trowel or a clean soft cloth.

10. Continue this procedure until wall is completed.

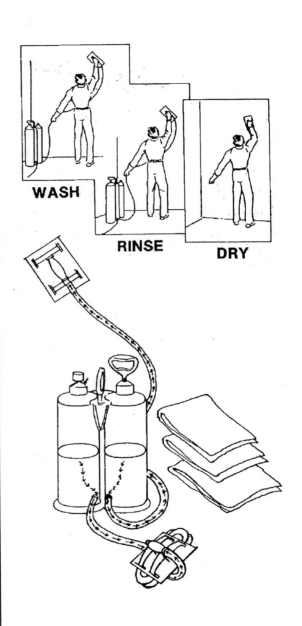

WASH

RINSE   **DRY**

PROCEDURE

11. Replace furniture and other wall mountings. Inspect work. There should be no streaks, surface contrasts or spots.

Remove towels from trowel and place in plastic liner for laundering. Wash, rinse and dry equipment. Rinse tanks and tubings. Dry. Return equipment to designated storage area.

VII. CLEANING ELEVATOR

PURPOSE: To improve sanitation of the environment, control bacteria and for appearance.

EQUIPMENT:

Utility cart
Counter brush and dustpan
Germicidal detergent
Cloths
Putty knife
Stainless steel cleaner
Electric floor machine
Buckets and Wringers on dolly (two)
Vacuum cleaner (wet and dry)
Four-foot ladder
Gloves
Buckets (two)
Sweeping tool—treated cloth

SAFETY PRECAUTIONS:

1. Take elevator to basement.

2. Put elevator out of order—turn off switch.

3. Do not prop doors open with sticks, buckets, or any other device.

4. Tracks of elevators must be cleaned daily (sometimes more frequently) so that door will open and close properly.

PROCEDURE

1. Assemble all equipment. Prepare solution. Take to designated area.

2. Put on gloves.

3. Vacuum walls, lights, vents, and tracks. Change brushes. Remove gum with putty knife.

4. Vacuum floor or dust with treated cloth.

5. Dip cloth in germicidal solution. Wring out. Spot wash wall areas. Rinse and dry. Wash and dry telephone and box. Wash doors inside and outside. Rinse and dry.

6. Polish all metal surfaces.

PROCEDURE

7. Wet mop floor. Follow wet mopping procedure.

8. Spray buff or buff floor area.

9. Release elevator and continue same procedures until all elevators are completed. Only one elevator should be put out of order at a time.

10. Clean equipment and return to designated storage area.

    NOTE: Once a week, thoroughly clean elevators :
    a. Vacuum thoroughly the walls, ceiling, floors, and tracks.

    b. Wash all walls (interior and exterior), knobs or buttons, control panel, ceiling, vents, ceiling light, telephone, and box. Rinse and dry.

    c. Polish all metal surfaces with recommended polishing agent.

    d. Light scrub floor area.

    e. Apply finish.

    f. Clean all equipment and return to designated storage area.

VIII. ENTRANCE AND LOBBY CLEANING

PURPOSE: to improve sanitation of the environment, to control bacteria and for appearance. The entrance of any building (whether it is a hospital, hotel, home, or business establishment) represents to visitors, potential patients, and others what the interior of the building will be. Therefore, it is very important that these areas are cleaned daily and policed several times each day. The entrance and lobby must be neat and clean at all times.

EQUIPMENT:

    Utility cart
    Gloves
    Cloths or Sponges
    Putty knife
    Plastic liners/bags
    Sifter and slit spoon
    Buckets (two)
    Electric floor machines
    Vacuum cleaner or
    Sweeping tool
    Glass cleaning agent
    Wet floor signs
    Buckets and Wringers on dolly (two)
    Mopheads and handles (two)
    Automatic scrubber
    Container for cigarette butts

Squeegee
Spray bottle
Deck brush
Broom and broom bags
Treated cloths
Germicidal detergent
Dustpan and Counter brush

SAFETY PRECAUTIONS:

1. Post wet floor signs.

2. Place equipment near wall area to avoid tripping when not in use.

3. Do not leave electric floor machine unattended and plugged in.

4. Wipe up spills immediately.

5. This operation should be performed during least traffic hours.

6. Clean only half of the lobby at a time. Move furniture.

7. Where urn screens are not in use, use sifter and slit spoon.

PROCEDURE

1. Assemble all equipment. Prepare solution. Take to lobby area.

2. Put on gloves.

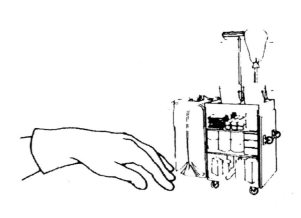

PROCEDURE

3. Clean front entrance. Take broom, counter brush, dustpan and plastic liner to outside area:

   a. Pick up large pieces of trash and place in plastic liner/bag.

   b. Sweep landing and/or steps.

   c. Continue sweeping sidewalk area.

   d. Take up debris with dustpan and counter brush.

4. Return equipment to utility cart.

5. Continue with the cleaning of the lobby:

   a. Post wet floor signs. Move furniture.

   b. Pick up large pieces of trash. Empty trash containers. Wash and dry containers inside and outside. Replace liner.

   c. Empty and wash ashtrays. Clean cigarette urns. Follow urn cleaning procedure.

   d. Take glass cleaning agent and clean cloths or squeegee and wash lobby windows and glass doors inside and outside. Wash any other glass in area at this time. Follow glass cleaning procedure.

   e. Check for cobwebs and remove.

   f. Dip cloth into germicidal solution. Wring out. Damp dust and dry all furniture, window sills, radiators/covers, and other items. Spot wash walls and around light switches. Return cloth frequently to germicidal solution for refreshing.

PROCEDURE

g. Vacuum or dust floor with sweeping tool or covered broom. Make sure to clean runners or mats—vacuum, hose off, mop or scrub.

h. Wet mop floor. Follow wet mopping procedure.

i. Return furniture to proper place and continue with procedure until lobby is completed.

6. Take equipment to utility room. Wash and dry. Return to designated storage area. Restock utility cart.

STAIRS AND STAIRWELLS,
PORCHES, AND BACK ENTRANCES
(Wet and Dry)

PURPOSE: To maintain a safe and sanitary environment, to control the spread of bacteria, and for appearance.

.

EQUIPMENT:

Utility cart
Buckets and Wringers on dolly (two)
Vacuum cleaner (back-pack or wet and
dry), or
Corn broom
Putty knife
Germicidal detergent
Scrub brush
Gloves
Mopheads and handles (two)
Broom bags
Counter brush
Wet floor or Out of order signs (two)
Cloths and Sponges

Buckets (two)
Plastic liner
Deck brush
Dustpan

SAFETY PRECAUTIONS:

1. Report loose treads and banisters and burned out light bulbs.

2. Set up caution signs at *each* doorway.

3. Leave a path open for traffic.

4. When cleaning wide stairs, clean half the width at a time. Leave a dry path for users.

5. Make sure back entrances and stairs are never blocked or cluttered with trash or broken furniture.

PROCEDURE

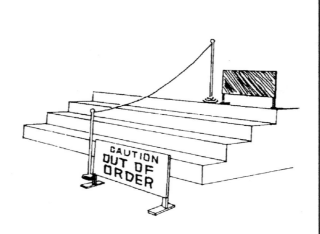

Dry Cleaning

1. Assemble equipment. Prepare solution. Take to assigned area.

2. Place caution sign on the bottom landing.

3. Take second sign, putty knife, and covered broom to top landing.

4. Place sign at top landing.

PROCEDURE

5. Remove any gum. Sweep top landing and work down the stairs. Sweep soil toward closed wall. Use single, continuous, horizontal strokes, and bring down to next step if back of step is closed. However, if back of steps are opened or if steps are opened on each side, counter brush and dustpan are used for this procedure. Sweep each step from both sides to center with counter brush and take up soil in dustpan.

6. Continue procedure until all steps are completed.

7. Sweep bottom landing. Take up trash with counter brush and dustpan. Place in trash bag on utility cart.

8. Dip cloth into germicidal solution. Wring out. Start at bottom and work to top of stairs. Damp dust banister, railing, spindles, radiator, window sills, and ledges.

9. Pick up sign. (Leave sign if wet procedure is being performed.)

10. Continue with the dusting procedure on the opposite side, working down until dusting is completed. (A vacuum may be used to reach difficult areas—ledges, radiators, or to remove cobwebs.)

11. Place caution signs on utility cart. Change cover on broom. Place cover in plastic liner/bag for laundering.

12. Continue to next assignment. If this is the last assignment, clean equipment and return to designated storage area.

PROCEDURE

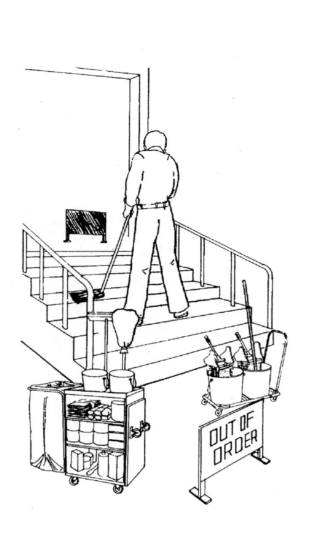

Wet Cleaning
(By Mop)

1. Assemble equipment. Prepare solution. Take to designated area.

2. Sweep stairway with a covered broom.

3. Place buckets on landing. Dip mop into germicidal solution. Press out excess water. Start at top landing and work down.

4. Mop a flight of stairs at a time. Turn mop frequently. Use mop strands to clean corners.

5. Dip second mop into rinse water. Wring out. Pick up soil and solution.

6. Continue this procedure until all steps and landings are completed.

7. Scrub bottom landing thoroughly. Use four-step wet mopping procedure. Apply cleaning solution. Pick up. Apply rinse water and pick up.

8. Take equipment to utility room. Wash, rinse, and dry. Return to designated storage area. Place dust cloths and mop-heads in plastic liner/ bag for laundering.

- - - - - - - - - - - - - - - - - -

Wet Cleaning
(By Hand)

1. Assemble equipment. Prepare solution. Take to assigned area.

2. Sweep stairway with covered broom.

PROCEDURE

3. Dip sponge into germicidal solution. Squeeze out excess water.

4. Apply solution to treads.

5. Scrub tread with hand scrub brush.

6. Pick up cleaning solution with germicidal solution sponge.

7. Rinse tread. Use second sponge.

8. Pick up rinse water.

9. Continue this process until all treads are completed.

10. Take equipment to utility room. Wash out sponges, brush, and buckets. Return to designated storage area.

Cleaning Wide Stairs
(Dry and Wet)

The procedure for cleaning wide stairs is the same as for narrow stairs with the following changes:

1. Only half of the width of wide steps is cleaned at a time.

2. The dusting procedure is performed before the sweeping procedure.

3. Wide steps are cleaned from bottom up.

ANSWER SHEET

TEST NO. ____________ PART ______ TITLE OF POSITION ______________________________
(AS GIVEN IN EXAMINATION ANNOUNCEMENT - INCLUDE OPTION, IF ANY)

PLACE OF EXAMINATION ______________________________ ______________________________ DATE ______
(CITY OR TOWN) (STATE)

RATING

USE THE SPECIAL PENCIL. MAKE GLOSSY BLACK MARKS.

1 A B C D E	26 A B C D E	51 A B C D E	76 A B C D E	101 A B C D E
2 A B C D E	27 A B C D E	52 A B C D E	77 A B C D E	102 A B C D E
3 A B C D E	28 A B C D E	53 A B C D E	78 A B C D E	103 A B C D E
4 A B C D E	29 A B C D E	54 A B C D E	79 A B C D E	104 A B C D E
5 A B C D E	30 A B C D E	55 A B C D E	80 A B C D E	105 A B C D E
6 A B C D E	31 A B C D E	56 A B C D E	81 A B C D E	106 A B C D E
7 A B C D E	32 A B C D E	57 A B C D E	82 A B C D E	107 A B C D E
8 A B C D E	33 A B C D E	58 A B C D E	83 A B C D E	108 A B C D E
9 A B C D E	34 A B C D E	59 A B C D E	84 A B C D E	109 A B C D E
10 A B C D E	35 A B C D E	60 A B C D E	85 A B C D E	110 A B C D E

Make only ONE mark for each answer. Additional and stray marks may be counted as mistakes. In making corrections, erase errors COMPLETELY.

11 A B C D E	36 A B C D E	61 A B C D E	86 A B C D E	111 A B C D E
12 A B C D E	37 A B C D E	62 A B C D E	87 A B C D E	112 A B C D E
13 A B C D E	38 A B C D E	63 A B C D E	88 A B C D E	113 A B C D E
14 A B C D E	39 A B C D E	64 A B C D E	89 A B C D E	114 A B C D E
15 A B C D E	40 A B C D E	65 A B C D E	90 A B C D E	115 A B C D E
16 A B C D E	41 A B C D E	66 A B C D E	91 A B C D E	116 A B C D E
17 A B C D E	42 A B C D E	67 A B C D E	92 A B C D E	117 A B C D E
18 A B C D E	43 A B C D E	68 A B C D E	93 A B C D E	118 A B C D E
19 A B C D E	44 A B C D E	69 A B C D E	94 A B C D E	119 A B C D E
20 A B C D E	45 A B C D E	70 A B C D E	95 A B C D E	120 A B C D E
21 A B C D E	46 A B C D E	71 A B C D E	96 A B C D E	121 A B C D E
22 A B C D E	47 A B C D E	72 A B C D E	97 A B C D E	122 A B C D E
23 A B C D E	48 A B C D E	73 A B C D E	98 A B C D E	123 A B C D E
24 A B C D E	49 A B C D E	74 A B C D E	99 A B C D E	124 A B C D E
25 A B C D E	50 A B C D E	75 A B C D E	100 A B C D E	125 A B C D E

ANSWER SHEET

TEST NO. _____ PART _____ TITLE OF POSITION _____

PLACE OF EXAMINATION _____ DATE _____

(CITY OR TOWN)   (STATE)

RATING

USE THE SPECIAL PENCIL.   MAKE GLOSSY BLACK MARKS.

	A B C D E		A B C D E		A B C D E		A B C D E		A B C D E
1	:: :: :: :: ::	26	:: :: :: :: ::	51	:: :: :: :: ::	76	:: :: :: :: ::	101	:: :: :: :: ::
2	:: :: :: :: ::	27	:: :: :: :: ::	52	:: :: :: :: ::	77	:: :: :: :: ::	102	:: :: :: :: ::
3	:: :: :: :: ::	28	:: :: :: :: ::	53	:: :: :: :: ::	78	:: :: :: :: ::	103	:: :: :: :: ::
4	:: :: :: :: ::	29	:: :: :: :: ::	54	:: :: :: :: ::	79	:: :: :: :: ::	104	:: :: :: :: ::
5	:: :: :: :: ::	30	:: :: :: :: ::	55	:: :: :: :: ::	80	:: :: :: :: ::	105	:: :: :: :: ::
6	:: :: :: :: ::	31	:: :: :: :: ::	56	:: :: :: :: ::	81	:: :: :: :: ::	106	:: :: :: :: ::
7	:: :: :: :: ::	32	:: :: :: :: ::	57	:: :: :: :: ::	82	:: :: :: :: ::	107	:: :: :: :: ::
8	:: :: :: :: ::	33	:: :: :: :: ::	58	:: :: :: :: ::	83	:: :: :: :: ::	108	:: :: :: :: ::
9	:: :: :: :: ::	34	:: :: :: :: ::	59	:: :: :: :: ::	84	:: :: :: :: ::	109	:: :: :: :: ::
10	:: :: :: :: ::	35	:: :: :: :: ::	60	:: :: :: :: ::	85	:: :: :: :: ::	110	:: :: :: :: ::

**Make only ONE mark for each answer.   Additional and stray marks may be
counted as mistakes.   In making corrections, erase errors COMPLETELY.**

	A B C D E		A B C D E		A B C D E		A B C D E		A B C D E
11	:: :: :: :: ::	36	:: :: :: :: ::	61	:: :: :: :: ::	86	:: :: :: :: ::	111	:: :: :: :: ::
12	:: :: :: :: ::	37	:: :: :: :: ::	62	:: :: :: :: ::	87	:: :: :: :: ::	112	:: :: :: :: ::
13	:: :: :: :: ::	38	:: :: :: :: ::	63	:: :: :: :: ::	88	:: :: :: :: ::	113	:: :: :: :: ::
14	:: :: :: :: ::	39	:: :: :: :: ::	64	:: :: :: :: ::	89	:: :: :: :: ::	114	:: :: :: :: ::
15	:: :: :: :: ::	40	:: :: :: :: ::	65	:: :: :: :: ::	90	:: :: :: :: ::	115	:: :: :: :: ::
16	:: :: :: :: ::	41	:: :: :: :: ::	66	:: :: :: :: ::	91	:: :: :: :: ::	116	:: :: :: :: ::
17	:: :: :: :: ::	42	:: :: :: :: ::	67	:: :: :: :: ::	92	:: :: :: :: ::	117	:: :: :: :: ::
18	:: :: :: :: ::	43	:: :: :: :: ::	68	:: :: :: :: ::	93	:: :: :: :: ::	118	:: :: :: :: ::
19	:: :: :: :: ::	44	:: :: :: :: ::	69	:: :: :: :: ::	94	:: :: :: :: ::	119	:: :: :: :: ::
20	:: :: :: :: ::	45	:: :: :: :: ::	70	:: :: :: :: ::	95	:: :: :: :: ::	120	:: :: :: :: ::
21	:: :: :: :: ::	46	:: :: :: :: ::	71	:: :: :: :: ::	96	:: :: :: :: ::	121	:: :: :: :: ::
22	:: :: :: :: ::	47	:: :: :: :: ::	72	:: :: :: :: ::	97	:: :: :: :: ::	122	:: :: :: :: ::
23	:: :: :: :: ::	48	:: :: :: :: ::	73	:: :: :: :: ::	98	:: :: :: :: ::	123	:: :: :: :: ::
24	:: :: :: :: ::	49	:: :: :: :: ::	74	:: :: :: :: ::	99	:: :: :: :: ::	124	:: :: :: :: ::
25	:: :: :: :: ::	50	:: :: :: :: ::	75	:: :: :: :: ::	100	:: :: :: :: ::	125	:: :: :: :: ::